Great is the Mystery of Faith

Great is the Mystery of Faith

Exploring faith through the words of worship

Paul Ferguson

CANTERBURY
PRESS
Norwich

First published in 2011 by the Canterbury Press Norwich
Editorial office
13–17 Long Lane
London EC1A 9PN, UK

Canterbury Press is an imprint of Hymns Ancient and Modern Ltd
(a registered charity)
13A Hellesdon Park Road, Norwich,
Norfolk NR6 5DR, UK

www.scm-canterburypress.co.uk

British Library Cataloguing in Publication data

A catalogue record for this book is available
from the British Library

978 1 84825 055 0

Typeset by the *Church Times*

Printed and bound in Great Britain by
CPI Antony Rowe, Chippenham

Contents

Acknowledgements

I am grateful to many people for their support in this project, particularly my wife, Penny, Canon Cathy Rowling and Dr Paula Gooder, who encouraged me to shape my first ideas into this book. I had the opportunity to write the draft during a period of study leave which the Archbishop of York, Dr John Sentamu, kindly granted me. During that time a number of colleagues, chiefly Canon Erik Wilson, generously covered my normal duties.

It is a privilege to be involved with the work of Readers in the Diocese of York as their Warden, and this book is dedicated to them and their ministry.

Paul Ferguson
Hutton Rudby, North Yorkshire
Christmas 2010

Introduction

About this book

The idea for this book was sparked off by some conversations I had with people at the end of church services. I'd ended a sermon or two with a comment on the lines of: 'The things we've been thinking about today are put perfectly in such-and-such a prayer that we say every week.' And at the end of the service someone would say, 'I never thought of that' or 'I hadn't realized that's what the prayer was about.' So the plan formed for this little book, to put a spotlight on the connections between words that are said in worship and the faith that stands behind them. And since many people who go to church services have stored up in their minds a wealth of words that are connected with faith, there seemed to be room for a book that would help unlock a little more of the meaning, and make a stronger bond between worship, our experience of God's love and our understanding.

So this book is mainly for people who are interested in faith and worship, but who haven't engaged in special theological study. I hope there is something here to help you in your praying or in being a follower of Jesus, and maybe something that will interest you by way of learning and thinking more about the Christian faith. I have tried to avoid too many technical terms, and to explain the ones that I do use.

I have taken a selection of words and texts that appear in the forms of service of the Church of England and other churches. Each chapter reflects on one text. There is a little cross-referencing between the chapters, but, apart from that, the plan of the book is that each chapter (or even a section of a chapter) can stand by itself as a text for study or meditation. At the end of each chapter is a question for thinking and reflection. So these chapters do not set out to be a series of commentaries in a uniform style: nor do they aim to be a history of our prayer books (although in some cases something of the story of a text is included for the sake of the bigger point I am making).

Many of the chapters touch on issues and questions that cannot be fully dealt with in a book this size, and about which many full and specialist books have been written. I can only ask you to forgive the oversimplifications that are inevitable here: there are some suggestions for more detailed reading at the end of the book.

The Bible

Much of the material that we use in worship is drawn directly or indirectly from the Bible. To a large extent, Christians pray through the Scriptures. So you will find quite a lot of Bible references and quotations in this book.

Bible quotations in this book are from the *New Revised Standard Version*, unless otherwise noted as the author's translation.

Any book that looks at texts from the Bible runs up against two questions: first, 'Who wrote different parts of it?'; and second, 'Did events and sayings reported in the Bible happen "just the way it says"?' As far as the first question is concerned, there are many books of the Bible for which we know little or nothing about the writer, or even who the writer actually was. It is generally agreed that Hebrews is by an unnamed and unknown author, and not by Paul, despite the heading in the *Authorized Version*. It has been suggested that Paul did not write all the other letters that bear his name (a question-mark hovers over the more essay-like Ephesians and Colossians in particular). There has been disagreement among scholars about how much of a hand Simon Peter might have had in writing the letters of Peter, how many people called John were involved in writing the New Testament, and so on. Intriguing as these questions are, they are not directly the concern of this book in its exploration of how the Church has taken themes from the Bible to undergird worship and faith. As far as worship is concerned, the body of Scripture is something of a 'given'. So, while not ignoring these questions about authorship, I will not go into them to an extent beyond what is necessary for the subject in hand.

To some degree the same applies to the second question. From the late 1700s, there was a growing movement among scholars, asking whether every account in the Bible was to be taken as true at face value, as literally factual. In earlier ages, the question had not generally arisen in the same way. As an example, we can probably assume that Thomas Cranmer and his contemporaries accepted without any significant doubt that there was an old man called Simeon who really did meet the infant Jesus, and who spoke the words that we now know as *Nunc dimittis*. The work of biblical scholars over the last couple of centuries or so have put a different possibility to us: that Luke composed the scene; that he was not recording an actual event, but giving his readers a word-picture in order to tell them truths in the form of a story. Many Christians believe what might be called the more conservative position because it is linked directly with their view of the nature and authority of Scripture. For others, the significance of what the writers are conveying is not affected by whether the scenes in the Gospels are exact literal reports. We might each take a range of different views on how far the 'Simeon scene' and others are reports or how far they are compositions. But, whatever our viewpoint, I hope that it does not detract from appreciating why, for example, *Nunc dimittis* is such an important element in worship, what its words can tell us, and how it can help us grow in faith.

Thinking about worship

Worship texts that are repeated day by day or week by week have great potential to feed us spiritually.

A reason for this is that the texts are based on words of the Bible, and, as a natural consequence of that, the words of worship are directly linked with the words of Scripture that address what it means to be a Christian believer and a disciple of Jesus Christ.

Then, formal or 'liturgical' services have a shape. They often take us on a spiritual or emotional journey through the time of worship. Services are not a jumble of ingredients thrown together 'any old how'. The individual texts fit into a dramatic shape.

Finally, liturgical worship has a balance between what is the *same* and what *changes*, or, in other words, a balance between *stability* and *flexibility*. When we attend such an act of worship, it is likely that we will hear at least some words that are special to that place or occasion. But the framework of the worship typically consists of carefully crafted texts that have been designed to be used over and over again, and which are well known to people worshipping in many different places, not just a single local congregation. Many Christians value this pattern of having a sizeable body of permanent or semi-permanent texts. When we say or hear the same words many times over a long period, they become familiar – and sometimes not only familiar but also some-how 'part of us'. It might be imagined that the words become like the water in a well: when we really need to draw on them, we don't have to search, we only have to reach.

Although this book is not written with a narrowly or exclusively Anglican audience in mind, it does draw on the liturgy of the Church of England. In the course of the history of the turbulent sixteenth and seventeenth centuries, from the first stirrings of reform in England in the early 1500s to the restoration of the monarchy in 1660, a living tradition of superbly crafted English religious texts was established. Even when we use newly composed texts from our own age, there is a recognizable 'Prayer Book heritage' which owes much to the scholarship, care and skill of Archbishop Thomas Cranmer (died 1556) and his contemporaries.

Tradition and heritage

In using the words tradition and heritage, we must not confuse them with a self-conscious reconstruction of the past. Walking through the church door should not feel like going on to the set of a television period drama. Tradition means literally *what is handed on*. Yes, part of tradition is valuing what the past has handed to us, but the other vital part of tradition is what we hand on to the future. The concerns that we bring to our prayers are in many ways different from those of 50, 100 or 400 years ago, and the future will bring new concerns that we cannot foresee. Faith is always fresh, and the Church is called to proclaim it in each generation, in terms that each generation will hear: God equips his Church for tomorrow's work, not for yesterday's.

Some chapters in this book are based on the *Book of Common Prayer* (1662) precisely for the reason that I believe the Prayer Book has the potential to be a framework for a lively faith that relates to a changing world, despite the turns of phrase being centuries' old. More specifically, many churches continue to hold services according to the Prayer Book, and it was important for this book to be a resource for people whose patterns of prayer and worship continue to be shaped by it. There are chapters based on *Common Worship* (1998–2000), reflecting some of the many words, phrases and ideas in it that have power to inspire us, and that are evidence that every age can produce fine prayers and liturgy. It is the experience of many churches, not only the Church of England, that we are enriched as believers and disciples through having forms of service that are both historic and contemporary.

Familiarity and freshness

There is something of a paradox in the way we treat the treasure store of the words of worship. On the one hand, the words we use or hear repeatedly have the wonderful potential to work themselves into our inner being. On the other hand – here is the disadvantage of familiarity – words that we hear and say repeatedly can lose their effect, because we stop paying attention to them. Part of the reason for this book is to help worshippers readjust, to think again about well-known words, and be encouraged afresh to live and work for God.

Part 1: Relationship with God

1

Worship and praise

O Lord, open our lips; and our mouth shall proclaim your praise

To begin with

There are so many words that we use in worship: and so many from which to choose a starting point. In Part 1 of this book we take up the theme of how God relates to humankind, and how that relationship is reflected in worship. After all, Christians believe that, when we pray and worship, we aren't talking pointlessly into empty space, but we are really communicating with God. And it's God's readiness to relate to humanity that provides the rationale for prayer. If God were aloof, and didn't care, then worship and prayer would have little point. But Christians believe that God's love is real and close.

'*O Lord, open our lips; and our mouth shall proclaim your praise.*' These two familiar lines from Psalm 51.15 speak about the inter-action between God and ourselves, the interplay of the very physical language about our mouth and lips, with words about God who is real but unseen. It's as if humanity is silent and unable to communicate until God breaks that silence and gives us the power of speech. These few words connect us with a big and diverse range of ideas and themes, and in the next pages we shall explore some of them.

When we use these words

These words have been familiar to millions of worshippers for many centuries. In many Christian churches, they come at, or near, the beginning of services of morning and evening prayer. The exact words may differ from one service to another: I have used them as they are found in *Common Worship*, but many people will be more familiar with the *Book of Common Prayer* version: 'O Lord, open thou our lips: and our mouth shall shew forth thy praise.'

Praise

It's easy to get into the habit of saying 'religious' words without pausing to think what they mean. The climax of this phrase is one of the most important and commonly used religious words: *praise*. Let's stop to think: what is praise, and why do we do it? The best definition I have found is that praise happens at any time and place, when people celebrate the fact that God exists and that God acts. The Bible frequently encourages us to praise, such as this instance from the letter to the Hebrews: 'Through him [Jesus], then, let us continually offer a sacrifice of praise to God, that is, the fruit of lips that confess his name' (Heb. 13.15). The words 'praise' and 'thanks' are often coupled together: acknowledging that God 'is' and that God 'does' goes hand in hand with being glad and grateful.

Part of praise, then, is being aware of God and giving attention to God. One way of doing that is to dedicate a slice of time, to stop the other things we are doing, and deliberately call God and his love to mind. There's no need to look for some measurable product or result from this. It's true, of course, that we might enjoy praising God; we may love the words and music and art that form our praise to God. But the reason for praise is not to make us, or other people, feel better or happier or excited. And it doesn't make much sense either to think of praise as a sort of entertainment for God, which the rest of us are allowed to overhear and enjoy. No – praise is celebration, pure and simple.

The definition of praise as a celebration of God who exists and acts prevents us limiting our idea of what praise is. The language and music of praise are often uplifting, but it is a big mistake to think that praise is something we can (or should) only do when we are in a particular mood. Associating praise with triumphant music can lead us into thinking of praise as something to do *when* we feel upbeat, and that when we feel differently praise is off the agenda. But that is to focus the rationale of praise on us and not on God. The basis for praise is God's existence, his love and everything he has done for humankind. That remains true whatever our emotional state happens to be. 'Alleluia' means 'praise the Lord', not 'I'm in a happy mood today'. It is therefore possible to say 'praise the Lord' and mean it, when for whatever reason we could not honestly say we felt happy. Praise is rooted in God's love, not in our changing experiences and emotions.

I'm not for a moment suggesting that we should put on a false and superficial show of happiness as a prerequisite for praising God. When we are in the middle of grief or big disappointment, it's important that we do not hide or deny our sadness. Praise helps us, even in these circumstances, to cling onto the claim that God exists for us and acts for us.

What praising God means for all our communication

When we pray, 'O Lord, open our lips; and our mouth shall proclaim your praise', we are asking for a gift from God, and we are making a pledge. It's not our opening bid in a bargain, but a promise that when God gives us the power of speech the first thing we will do is to return a token of his gift to him. Here then is another big theme that these two short lines unlock for us: we honour God in how we use the things he gives us. If we offer a token back to him, what does that mean for the way we use the rest of his gifts?

We encounter the idea of a token offering elsewhere, in the context of the harvest festival. In ancient Jewish celebrations of the harvest the farmer would bring the first fruits of the crop (Ex. 23.19; Deut. 26.1–11) to acknowledge that the gift of food comes from God: in other words, God is the real owner of the land and of what it produces. There is no suggestion that by offering God the part of something it is possible to buy off his interest in the rest. The principle is this: if a small part is holy and dedicated to God, then the whole must be used in a way that honours God and accords with the values that spring from faith.

In promising that 'our mouth shall proclaim your praise' we are saying that we will use *all* our powers of communication in ways that acknowledge those powers as God's gift to us – not by self-consciously peppering our phone calls and text messages with religious words; but in all our communication we will try to witness to what it means to live as a follower of Jesus.

When we have carried out our promise to praise God, the effect of giving that token needs to overflow from worship and become the background of everything else we speak and write. If we pause for a moment we will see why this is so important. A huge amount of what it means to be a Christian disciple relates to how we interact with other people; and a great proportion of that inter-action takes the form of words, both written and spoken. Our powers of speech mean that we are able to say not only words that are good or holy or helpful but also words that can hurt, provoke and destroy. And we do not even have to use words. A cold silence can break a relationship, a smile to a stranger can express warmth and welcome. Politeness can mask an abusive attitude.

Used for good or for ill, our communication often has an influence over situations and people greater than we imagine. Offering the 'first fruits' of our speech to God in worship and praise reminds us that we are stewards of the gift of communica-tion. An example from the New Testament can help us here. Paul wrote to the Christians in Colossae reminding them to put behind them the kind of behaviour and communication that belonged to their former lives: 'anger, wrath, malice, slander, and abusive language' (Col. 3.8). Paul says that the way that they use their communication is part and parcel of their new life in Christ: 'you have died, and your life is hidden with Christ in God ... you have stripped off the old self with its practices and have clothed yourselves with the new self' (Col. 3.3, 9–10). So there is a direct link between our communication and what it means to follow our calling with integrity as Jesus' disciples. And in a world where communication is changing so fast – many of us have a flood of words and information on to our computer screens every day – it's ever more important that we remember that our ability to communicate is God-given. As we pledge to use *part* of our communication to praise him, we are called to use *all* of it to honour him.

There is worship everywhere and every day

'O Lord, open our lips; and our mouth shall proclaim your praise' is said in many places and in many languages around the world, day in day out, as part of daily prayer. When we pray these words, we are part of a great movement of worship that crosses boundaries of time and space.

These words are said on days of great celebration, as well as when the drama of Holy Week is reaching its sorrowful climax on Good Friday. Other words that are used in worship change with the season, but these do not. It is the same on every day of the year. This is itself saying something important. However our situation or state of mind may vary from one day to another, the love of God is always close and the fact that he acts is always true. Each day brings the potential for praise. Every day God's Church prays, 'O Lord, open our lips', as witness to his loving relationship with humanity, and in thanksgiving for the God-given ability to respond through what we say and what we do.

Praising in the plural

The verse of the Bible from which these words are borrowed is Psalm 51.15: 'O Lord, open my lips, and my mouth will declare your praise.' Here the prayer is in the singular: '*my* lips, *my* mouth'. Many Churches have kept that singular 'my' for use in daily prayer – even the first English prayer book, in 1549, did the same. But in

7

1552, perhaps to emphasize that the whole congregation was included, it was changed to the plural '*our* lips, *our* mouth', and that form has been used in Anglican churches ever since. It's a happy accident in that, even when people use this form of prayer with no one else present, it is a reminder that no one really prays alone. There *is* an 'us': an invisible congregation of which every praying person is a part. There are millions who will be praying and praising somewhere each day, and there is the whole company of heaven to whom we are joined in worship. Knowing this is a great encouragement, because whenever we worship and praise, and especially when we use words that other people are also using, we are never truly isolated.

Our praise and prayer

Where might these thoughts lead us? What can we do to refresh our own pattern of praise and prayer?

The Church's 'official' forms of daily prayer have a great deal to offer as a foundation for our individual prayer. Many resources exist to help us cultivate a habit of daily prayer, but using the full authorized forms of morning and evening prayer – though to be commended – will not suit everybody. Instead, some may prefer to start in easy stages. Any pattern of praise and prayer is first and foremost about giving attention to God, and to his love for humanity. It's about saying 'yes' to God. You might find it helpful to start with some of the elements of daily worship – a psalm, readings, canticle and prayers, perhaps. If you use a computer you'll be able to get all of these very easily, for every day, simply by putting 'daily prayer' into a search engine. But it's important not to get bogged down in words. One mistake is to race through the words if the set readings for the day seem long. Another is to think that unless we can find *just* the right words our worship isn't worthy; or to assume that worship must be expressed in words (it needn't!). Even going no further than saying our key phrases from this chapter, 'O Lord, open our lips; and our mouth shall proclaim your praise', and then really taking time to think about how *today* can be a day for honouring God in our words and actions, is authentically praise and prayer. Our pattern of prayer needs to be realistic for us. Sometimes changing the way we pray, maybe for a period of time, helps to keep it fresh. Or it could be that there is someone in your community that would value having you as a prayer companion, either regularly or occasionally. The chief thing is to have some space (quality is more important than quantity) in which you can celebrate God's love, aloud or in the silence of the heart.

To think about further

How can I cultivate communication that is both honest and compassionate: at home, in the church context and elsewhere?

Has my pattern of prayer 'grown with me' over the years? When did I last think seriously about my prayer life?

2

Meeting God in Scripture

This is the word of the Lord: Thanks be to God

When someone says, 'This is the word of the Lord', at the end of a Bible reading, we respond, 'Thanks be to God', without any hesitation. What are we actually giving thanks for, when we say those words? Why do we only say them at the end of readings from the Bible? Could it be that we *have* simply got into a habit of making that response, and that it is little more than a way of registering that a reading is finished? And while there are some Bible passages that we can immediately and happily say 'thanks' for, what about the more difficult ones? Would we sympathize with the student who came to the end of an account of battle and murder, and said with his voice rising in disbelief, '*This* is the word of the *Lord*?'

Why Scripture?

The words of Scripture are a means through which God meets us and speaks to us. The Old Testament (the Hebrew Scriptures) focuses on God's dealings with the Jewish people, and the New Testament is centred on the figure of Jesus of Nazareth. Christians believe that the same God who chose and called the Jews to be his people, and who met women, children and men in the person of Jesus of Nazareth, meets us now through the words that we read and hear.

So there is an important marker to put down at the outset. The Christian faith is rooted in the relationship between God and humanity, through Jesus Christ. The Bible is the written foundation of Christianity. But the Bible is not itself the essence of

Christianity. It would be possible to have Christianity without the Bible (even though it would be a very different kind of Christianity), but it would not be possible to have Christianity without Jesus Christ. The Bible witnesses to Jesus, and not the other way round.

And that is why there are different approaches to interpreting the Bible among Christians. Most Christians would agree that it's not necessary to take a very conservative approach to Scripture in order to believe that God reveals truths about himself through words. Christians share the conviction that God uses the Bible to tell us about himself, and that it has a standing and authority that no other collection of writings does: that's what we mean when we say that it is 'the word of the Lord'. The Bible is the reason why Christianity is not shakily built on hearsay and legend. The Bible is very diverse: it is made up of over 60 different kinds of writings – history, poetry, prophecy, letters, story – produced over hundreds of years. Its writers tackle subjects in different and distinctive styles. But being diverse does not mean that they are fragmentary or disjointed. There is a single story – the story of God's dealings with humankind – running through the Bible. When we speak about the Bible as one body of writing, it doesn't mean that all the parts are alike, but it does mean that they belong together.

Whenever we read or hear the Bible, we are in touch with the times and places and cultures in which it was produced. But the Bible's message or relevance are not locked into faraway countries and past ages – anything but! The books of the Bible make more sense, not less, when we think about the setting in which they were written. We describe the Bible as 'timeless' meaning that it has a message for all times and that it even tells us something about eternity, but it is also 'of a time', bearing the marks of the setting in which its books were written. So it is one thing to say, 'Thanks be to God', for it is our Scriptures that show how faith developed and how writers variously addressed important quesions.

It's important to keep this big picture in our sights, even when we hear a short passage of the Bible read in church: it may be one part of one book, from one or other of the two testaments that make up the Bible that we are hearing, but it is part of a bigger story.

Thanks be to God for two Testaments

It's regrettable that for some Christians, the Old Testament is disappearing off their spiritual radar. The reason is partly to do with our patterns of churchgoing and what happens in church services. A couple of generations ago, a fairly large proportion of Anglican churchgoers, for example, would have gone regularly to morning or evening prayer (Matins or Evensong) on Sundays, where they would have heard a reading from the Old Testament and the New. Many now attend a weekly Eucharist with a scheme of readings that consists of an Old Testament reading, a Psalm, a reading from the New Testament and a Gospel passage. In practice, perhaps for the sake of saving time, a lot of churches drop the Old Testament reading. But there's a strong case for Christians reading and hearing the Old Testament, which means not being too ready to cut readings from it at Sunday services. There's a better answer to the question 'Why do we read the Old Testament?' than 'Because it's there.'

The Old Testament, the Scripture that Christians owe to the heritage of Judaism, comprises the story of God building a nation, making himself known to it, and giving it a special responsibility among the other peoples of the world. Much of the Old Testament is a record of what happened in and to the nation: its triumphs and disasters, the hopes and fears of the people, the wisdom and the mistakes of its leaders. Some of the stories are intensely personal. We read about the kind of people they were when at war and in love, at prayer and building a society. The theme of how God's relationship with his people touches all aspects of their life, individually and together, runs all the way through the Old Testament. That goes some way to explaining why there are parts of the Old Testament that from our cultural perspective we may not have included in an exclusively 'religious' book. But we don't have to sanitize the Bible and cut out the parts that aren't in line with our twenty-first-century outlook: in fact, doing so would be a mistake. Embracing the Old Testament as Scripture does, however, mean taking the journey and experience of the people of Israel seriously, both in their own right and as the background for the story of Jesus.

It's not altogether surprising that Christians often have some difficulty in deciding how to get to grips with the Old Testament. The problem is not helped by the fact that the description 'Old Testament' is too often (and thoughtlessly) used to imply 'primitive' – as if the Hebrew Scriptures are all about revenge carried out by God or people, lists of obscure rules, and never-ending wars. That hardly encourages Christians to see them as a body of writings to love and learn from, and it is a terrible distortion of the whole spectrum of the Old Testament, and of its picture of God. Granted, Christians believe that the historical events of Jesus' life, death and resurrection move the state of the world on from how it was before, and in that sense 'from old to new'. Christians believe that themes revealed in the Old Testament are transposed into a new dimension in Jesus: but that very definitely does *not* mean that the Old Testament became redundant once the age of the New arrived. Many places in the New Testament encourage Christians to have respect for Judaism and the Jewish Law: look, for example, at many of the words of Jesus, the second half of Romans, and Galatians. The Old Testament is far more than a long overture to the New, and it has value and integrity as Scripture in its own right.

There's another aspect to mention, which stems from the fact that the Old Testament is the document of a nation. In that respect, it is unlike the New Testament, which is set in the life of the early Church – a body of people from many nations who as yet had no official position in society, and no access to political power. That difference is the reason why most of the material in the Bible that amounts to a call for public justice, including provision for the poor and for foreigners, is in the pages of the Old Testament.

The New Testament does not deny that aspect of the Old or conflict with its message. It's sometimes said that Christianity is concerned with what individuals do, rather than how society functions, but that is to forget a significant element of how the Bible came to be written.

Again and again, the Old Testament records the meeting between God and his people. It includes the histories, and the words of the prophets who spoke to the people from the perspective of being commissioned by God. As well as the Psalms, it gives us many other poetic passages. And in its regulations for society we see how an ancient people addressed the question of how a nation should live 'under God'. God showed them that they had a destiny, and that alongside their relationship with him there came unique responsibilities. The God of love, peace and justice, the God who forgives and restores, meets us as we experience the 'Law, prophets and writings' that make up the Hebrew Scriptures.

Encountering God in the New Testament

Every time we read from the New Testament, it is an invitation to imagine what life was like for the first generation of Christians, as they came to terms with the belief that Jesus was risen from the dead. God had done something utterly new. Life was no longer the same. There's a crackling excitement and conviction that comes not only through *what* they wrote but also *how* they wrote.

Their writings were fresh and distinctive. They wrote about things that Jesus had done, but they did not write diaries or biographies. They recorded things he had said, but they did not put together books containing quotations alone. They expressed some of what they wanted to tell in the form of stories, but they did not write books of heroic tales. They included instructions about how people should live under God, but they did not produce a rule book. What they did was to write about Jesus as the pivot around whom the whole of human history revolves; and they wrote about his death and resurrection as the events which mean more than anything else that has happened since the world began or that will happen before it ends.

They used words and phrases from the Old Testament, because they were sure that God had a single plan for humanity that stretched back to the beginning of time, a plan to which the Old Testament writers bore witness. They put stories, hymns, word-pictures, all sorts of arguments, visionary scenes and much more into their writings. Often their words push at the limit of what words can convey.

Everything that is in the New Testament is there because it is part of the message of Jesus Christ, or part of the testimony of the early Church under the Spirit of God. It's as if each one of the writers is inviting us to look at how much God loves humanity, and how much he loves us. 'If anyone is in Christ, there is a new creation,' wrote Paul: 'everything old has passed away; see, everything has become new!' (2 Cor. 5.17).

Keeping our relationship with Scripture fresh

The Bible has the power to be compelling and exciting. If we are to appreciate God's gift of Scripture fully – the good news of Jesus Christ, and God telling us about himself through the words of the Bible writers – then it's important that our engagement with it remains fresh and lively. If our experience of the Bible often leaves us puzzled or bored, it's time to do something about it.

For most people who encounter the Bible directly, it is usually in the context of church services. That's fine! But there's a snag. In church we usually read short passages. The people who put the scheme of readings (called the lectionary) together did their best to choose readings that are suited to this kind of delivery. But many of those short passages only make the *best* sense when we see them as part of a whole, and sometimes we need to engage with Scripture at a bigger scale than 'church-size pieces'. To see this, I suggest that you sit and read through a large chunk – a few chapters at least – of John's Gospel. To do that is to experience the sequence of big 'set piece' scenes where Jesus has a conversation with one or more people, during which he reveals an important truth about himself. Reading at speed may mean missing some of the detail, but once in a while at least that doesn't matter. It's exhilarating to be carried along by the momentum of the Gospel, moving from one of John's scenes to the next. It shows something of the Gospel, and how John pictures Jesus, that we don't get from the same material delivered in the form of short, disconnected readings. As well as John's Gospel, you can do the same with the other Gospels; other parts of the Bible for which this way of reading can work well are the first half of Romans or the whole of Philippians. Or, for a 'Christian beginner's course' in a few pages, you might enjoy 1 Peter.

Another way altogether of reading the Bible is to do the exact opposite. Take a short – maybe very short – passage, even a single verse, and read it over and over again, letting it sink in, and wait for it to say something to you. Give it time; give it space. And yet another way is to choose a scene, perhaps one where Jesus is talking with some people. Imagine yourself in the scene. If there are several characters, take one part and then another. What did you notice? How did you feel? Did the passage come alive for you in a new way?

These are all ways of reading the Bible without any outside help. But of course there are Bible reading aids available if you would find them helpful. There are commentaries in many different styles and Bible reading notes. You can shop around and find some in a style that is right for you.

If the Bible passages you hear in church are puzzling, it might help to get hold of a different translation from the one that is being read, and look the passages up in it. Some translations have a wonderful style but it's at the price of many of the sentences being hard to take in, especially in the New Testament letters. The Authorized or 'King James' Version was an incredible achievement, but in the 400 years since it was produced the meaning of some English words has changed, and furthermore the understanding that scholars have of the Bible's languages, Hebrew and Greek, as well as the study of early manuscripts, have moved on a long way. And that itself is a hint that when we say, 'Thanks be to God', we are celebrating the work of Bible scholars, translators and interpreters – for the work of unfolding the Scriptures is work that is never finished.

There is so much to thank God for in the gift of the written word of Scripture. The Bible with its many ingredients has been sifted and recited and loved and learnt over the centuries. We are fortunate enough to have the Bible available easily and cheaply, and in our own language – things that we should never take for granted. And reading and hearing the Bible is as much of a great adventure as ever it was.

We must never lose the perspective that at the heart of the Christian Scriptures is the person of Jesus. To read and reread the Bible is to honour and treasure the writings through which God reveals himself, and it binds the Christian community together around Jesus himself. Reading the Bible creatively, imaginatively, humbly and thankfully is to be part of a movement under God. It is an exciting adventure which has power to challenge, surprise, call and renew us.

To think about further

The Church in Wales gives this optional form of thanksgiving to use at the end of a reading, which borrows words from Revelation 2.7: 'Hear what the Spirit is saying to the Church. Thanks be to God.'

How strongly do we feel the Spirit of God speaking to us through Scripture: in worship, in group study, at other times?

When have we felt this most powerfully?

3

God knows me inside out

The Collect for Purity

Before we look at the prayer that is the subject of this chapter, let us think about some words from a psalm to set the mood. There are many psalms that express the close relationship between God and an individual person, but none so much as Psalm 139. Here are a few phrases from it:

> O LORD, you have searched me and known me.
> You know when I sit down and when I rise up … [you] are acquainted with all my ways.
> Even before a word is on my tongue, O LORD, you know it completely.
>
> Such knowledge is too wonderful for me; it is so high that I cannot attain it.

This psalm is full of wonder at how intimate God's knowledge of us is. God knows us in a way that no human person does. God's knowledge is not a 'supercharged version' of the closeness of a friend, partner or parent. And God knows us more closely, and in a different way, even compared to how we know ourselves. It is, as the psalm writer says, 'too wonderful', but God knows what we do, what we think, what our unspoken words are. God knew about our physical selves even before we were formed: 'you knit me together in my mother's womb'. This God is everywhere: 'Where can I flee from your presence?' – we cannot escape from God. But by the same token it means that, wherever we are, we can find God there: in the sky or the sea. Even, the writer says, in Sheol, the name that Jews gave to the shadowy realm which they pictured as the dwelling place of the dead, 'your hand shall lead me, and your right hand shall hold me fast'.

To whom all hearts are open

The mood of the psalm is very much that it's a *positive* thing that God knows us and all about us. And that's an important idea to hold onto, especially when we give our particular attention to God and begin a time of prayer and worship. It's the spirit of the prayer which we are looking at in this chapter: a prayer that comes near the beginning of the Communion service, and that is normally called the Collect for Purity. It starts like this:

> Almighty God, to whom all hearts are open, all desires known, and from whom no secrets are hidden …

This first phrase isn't there to tell God something he knows already. It is in itself a prayer in which we acknowledge something important. It sets the scene, and reminds us of the relationship between God and humanity. The fact that our hearts and desires are open and known to God is simply 'how it is'. To say that our hearts are open to God is to recognize that God knows our thoughts and our motives and all the things that drive us (this prayer is using the Bible's meaning of 'heart' to refer to our thoughts as well as our emotions). In a way that we can't comprehend, God knows the whole truth about us (remember the description 'too wonderful' in the psalm again). God's knowledge includes the things about ourselves that we don't see, those that we find difficult to acknowledge and face, those that we wish weren't how they are, and those we would like to hide. This prayer doesn't accuse us of deliberately trying to hide our 'true selves' from God. But we *can* find ourselves habitually not having the courage to see ourselves, our actions and our motives as they really are. So even in the very first words of this prayer, and before we come to the 'asking' part of it, we are taking a very big spiritual step. That is to embrace the truth that God knows all about us – to put ourselves, if you like, in the position of the writer of Psalm 139.

That leads us a step further, because it makes no sense to acknowledge to God that he knows everything about us, unless we then have courage under God to know ourselves better. Straight away we can see that there is a demanding and serious aspect to this. But there is also huge reassurance – and here are three reasons why that is so.

The first is that because there is no point in any attempt at concealing anything from God, and no possibility that there are secrets hidden from him, there's no point in wasting mental and spiritual energy trying to cling on to whatever we must (and probably will) come to realize is a half-truth or untruth. So let God be God, and let the truth be the truth.

The second follows: if God is going to work within us and through us, that has to be through the real person that we are, not a figment of our own invention. We're putting up a needless barrier against whatever it is that God wants to do with us, if we don't open the 'real me' to the love and the grace and the power of God.

And the third aspect is that if God knows our hearts and our secrets then there is something else that he knows – and that is our potential, what we can do and what can be with the help of the Holy Spirit. He knows the capacity we have for being his co-workers, ambassadors and representatives. If Psalm 139 is positive about God's knowledge and presence, then we need to be positive about the fact that 'no secrets are hidden' from him. We must not hear those words *only* in a sense that God knows our flaws. People with a religious faith can find themselves in a state of mind where they say, 'I haven't got it in me to do much for God', or, 'I'm not good enough'. We can find ourselves repeating the words of Peter when he was coming to terms with who Jesus was, and could not cope with the realization: 'Go away from me, Lord, for I am a sinful man!' (Luke 5.8). But Jesus' response was to reassure Peter and draw him to be with him in his work: 'Do not be afraid' (Luke 5.10). Just as it's possible for us to fool ourselves into hiding our faults, it's also possible for us to ignore the potential that God sees in us.

The inspiration of your Holy Spirit

Our prayer goes on to ask:

> Cleanse the thoughts of our hearts by the inspiration of your Holy Spirit, that we may perfectly love you, and worthily magnify your holy name.

In day-to-day speech we've given 'inspiration' a rather romantic meaning: a man catches sight of a field of daffodils and comes home with a world-famous poem in his head. That isn't really what is meant here. Spirit means breath, and in-spiration means breathing. So our prayer is carrying the theme of the intimate relationship between God and ourselves a stage further. This is a prayer that God's Spirit will breathe in us and through us. Yes, it's picture language. We are asking God's Being to be intertwined with our being. We are inviting God into our minds and into every aspect of our lives, both what is expressed and what remains hidden. This phrase in the Collect for Purity means far more than 'give us some religious feelings, and help us to concentrate on God for the next hour'. It *is* a prayer for cleansing and, as such, to be guarded from anything that distracts us from worship. But it's a prayer for a deep clean rather than a quick dust. It means 'purify our thoughts, our habits of how we think about everything; and bring us in every aspect of our being into line with your will'.

So it is that we offer our whole mental and spiritual selves to God, as we pray 'that we may perfectly love you'. That echoes one of the key passages in the Bible, where Moses makes a speech reminding the people of Israel of all that God has done for them, and setting out their obligation to live in accordance with God's commands. Moses says, 'You shall love the Lord your God with all your heart, and with all your soul, and with all your might' (Deut. 6.4–5). To pray that we may perfectly love God is to pray that the relationship between God and ourselves may be deepened. There is a bond between the love that we express for God in our worship and the love that we are called to show for him in the whole of our lives, 'heart and soul and might' – practically and every day, not only in the confines of church buildings and service times.

A prayer of preparation

So far we have looked at the themes of the intimate relationship between God and ourselves. When we pray this prayer, we are asking God for that relationship to become stronger. Why is this prayer particularly significant at the start of worship? Part of the answer is to be found in the story of how we got this prayer.

The English version that we know is a translation of a medieval Latin prayer. It comes from the order for Mass known as the Sarum rite, which is the form of service that was used in southern England and some other places, up to the time of the Reformation.[1] Archbishop Cranmer and his colleagues would have known it well. It was one of the prayers that the priest said before Mass started. In fact the preparation for the Sarum Mass took quite a long time and could not easily be hurried. It included a hymn and a psalm, the Lord's Prayer and separate confessions by the priest and servers, as well as this prayer. It seems that there was something deliberate and purposeful in all this: it was impossible to rush into the start of Mass. So this prayer has its beginnings as a prayer of recollection, of calming down, of getting rid of the mental clutter. The first official English translation of the prayer came at the beginning of the order for Holy Communion in the

---

1 It seems that the prayer was also used outside the context of the Mass, because what we could call an 'unofficial' medieval English translation of it appears at the beginning of the religious writing called *The Cloud of Unknowing* that was written in the 1300s.

first English Prayer Book in 1549, and it has been part of Anglican liturgy ever since. Some forms of service still bear a trace of how this prayer was used in the Middle Ages, by including a direction (or 'rubric') that the priest is supposed to say this prayer alone. But over many years, in many churches, the custom grew up of the whole congregation saying this prayer together (we could call that a piece of constructive disobedience to the exact instructions!) and *Common Worship* Order One does now set the prayer to be said by the whole congregation. It has become *everyone's* prayer, and not only the priest's prayer.

Common Worship gives this prayer the title 'Prayer of Preparation'. It would be impossible to expect congregations to break the habit of calling it the Collect for Purity. But it's no bad thing to pick up that preparation theme, and to remember that this prayer started as a part of how people got ready to begin a service. In medieval times that involved a long ceremony, of a kind that we would not imitate today. All the same, the Collect for Purity is a prayer that we can treasure – and maybe make better use of – as an antidote to busyness. It is not one extra item to be fitted into the service, but a prayer that creates a space, and so helps our other prayers. There may be occasions when it is worth underlining the point, by keeping a decent pause before saying this prayer, so that it does not become swamped by all the other things that can tug at our attention at the beginning of worship.

Worship in spirit and truth

If worship is going to have integrity, it has to be based on truth – truth about God and truth about ourselves. To explore what that might mean, let us look at another passage in the Bible: the long scene (John 4.1–42) that is built around the conversation between Jesus and a Samaritan woman at a well. One of the subjects that the woman brings up is whether it was the Jews, or their rivals the Samaritans, who worshipped God in the right way and in the right place. For those peoples, the question will have been of burning importance, as important to them as any of today's theological issues might be to us. Jesus moves beyond the question as the woman poses it and says, '[T]he hour is coming, and is now here, when the true worshippers will worship the Father in spirit and truth, for the Father seeks such as these to worship him' (John 4.23). Worship worth the name is built on a profound relationship between God and humanity, which John sees as centred in Jesus himself – and nothing else will do. Having what people might think of as the correct physical setting, location, words and actions is no substitute. If we have a wonderful heritage of buildings and words to use in worship, they can be a real blessing: but they do not themselves make a relationship with God. And if ever we become protective of the particular way that we worship, or for that matter of any particular policy in relation to church life, we need to remember this dialogue between Jesus and the woman: because Jesus takes the opportunity to challenge the idea of what is 'correct' in worship, and lifts it on to a different plane. When we pray that we may more fully love God and magnify his name, we must not secretly congratulate ourselves that we 'do things right here': rather, we are offering ourselves to be changed, and to have our understanding of worship transformed from the time-bound and earth-bound into something far more glorious.

The Collect for Purity reminds us that alongside the realism of our failures and faults and shortcomings is the realism of the wonderful possibilities that God can bring into being. And it's a prayer that we can give enough room in our busy minds and lives, and enough space for the Spirit of God, to be renewed, refreshed, and reassured.

To think about further

How far do we find the idea that God knows everything about us difficult or comforting? Why?

4

Being sorry and being forgiven

The Confession

A friend came to visit. 'What's that prayer you Anglicans have about being miserable?' she asked. I puzzled for a while and then we worked out that the prayer she was talking about is the Confession in the morning and evening service (Matins and Evensong) in the *Book of Common Prayer*. Our friend knows us well enough (I hope) not to think that we spend all our time being 'gloomy for God'. But a lot of people probably do think that the Christian faith has a lot to do with being 'down'. It's part of that general idea that religion is bound up with the command (and notice the stern use of *Authorized Version* language) 'thou shalt not'.

But a lot of church services *do* include a Confession, and we *do* talk a fair amount about sin. So let's explore what this is all about, and let's have the Prayer Book Confession at our elbow while we do it.

Sin

The concept of sin goes back a very long way, and it's deeply rooted in the Old Testament. At one level the principle is simple: God has given humans standards to live by, and we fail. In Deuteronomy, the Ten Commandments are pictured as the basis of the binding two-way ('covenant') relationship between God and the people of Israel, and it is by God's authority that Moses gives all the laws that they are to observe (Deut. 4.13–14). Any failure to keep the commandments and the laws is sin, for which the Bible languages of Hebrew and Greek both use words that mean to 'miss' or 'fail'.[2] Already in the Old Testament we can see that sin is understood, not solely in terms of breaking specific rules, but as failure to live in accord with God's all-encompassing will: which is an aspect of Judaism that Christians don't always appreciate. When a scribe asked Jesus to say which was the greatest commandment in the Law, Jesus actually chose two – the commands to love the one true God (Deut. 6.5), 'and your neighbour as yourself' (Lev. 19.18). Christians sometimes refer to this episode (Matt. 22.34–40) as 'Our Lord's summary of the Law', but Jesus wasn't inventing new words and ideas; he was reflecting a very strong strand in the Jewish tradition. 'On these two commandments hang all the law and the prophets,' said Jesus, that is, the core of how to live in accordance with God's plan does not consist of a long list of rules. Rather, the individual commands all flow out of the relationship between God and humanity, which in turn must be reflected in dealings between humans: a principle which is spelt out most obviously in the Ten Commandments themselves (Ex. 20.1–17; Deut. 5.6–21). And, as Jesus pointed out, it is not just our outward actions that are measured by this principle, but our desires and intentions as well (Matt. 5.21–28).

When we think that God has intentions for how we think and act, and about the kind of mindset that we would need in order to be in tune with them, there is an inescapable conclusion: we can't manage to live up to the standard, the divine ideal. So if sin is failure to do what God intends, then it is everywhere. There's sin in our failure to care for others, sin in our casual attitude to the planet, as well as in unethical financial and political dealings. It's there in the individual and corporate failures in the Church. It's hypocritical to think of sin as something that other people do, because it's in our own minds, on our own lips and on our own hands.

And because sin – a failure to live and love as God would have

---

2 *Hātā* (with a rough 'h') in Hebrew and *hamartano* in Greek.

us do – reaches into every part of life, it's important that we don't allow the idea of sin, and the way we use the word, to be narrowed down or trivialized. To take the most obvious example, it's simply wrong to speak as if sin is only about sex. No: sin is a serious, damaging, turning away from God, and it is not confined to any one facet of human life. There is an objective quality about sin. It is not a measure of how we feel. Sin is a description of a broken relationship with God. We need to see this in a much more radical way than breaking rules: it's about our habits of thought, our outlook and attitude. We need to look beyond a 'catalogue' approach to sins (a list of 'bad things' we might have done), and see the seriousness of our tendency to pull away from God. The individual events in our lives, the 'sins', are important for us to recognize for what they are, but there is more to *sin* than *sins*.

Confession

Confession is what happens when we acknowledge that our relationship with God is askew, and come to him so that it can be mended. In our church services we have got forms of words that we use: words that are a way of carrying the truth that we are expressing. This is how the Confession in the traditional order for morning and evening prayer begins:

> Almighty and most merciful Father, we have erred, and strayed from thy ways like lost sheep. We have followed too much the devices and desires of our own hearts. We have offended against thy holy laws. We have left undone those things which we ought to have done; and we have done those things which we ought not to have done; and there is no health in us.

The image of straying sheep is a familiar figure of speech in the Bible for people who are directionless and adrift from God. In the Christian context it immediately suggests as well the picture of Christ the good shepherd (John 10.11), and Jesus' parable of the lost sheep in which the owner is overjoyed when the sheep is found. In the same way, says Jesus, there is 'joy in heaven' over a sinner who comes back to God (Luke 15.3–7). So, behind these words is a hint that, while wandering from God is a serious matter, the situation is not beyond rescue. We'll come back to that later.

'Devices and desires' is a two-pronged expression about both what we want and also the things that we have deliberately planned and devised. The prayer doesn't say that wanting and planning anything is in itself wrong, and being a Christian doesn't mean that we must constantly deprive ourselves of enjoyable things: but if we have 'followed too much' what is in our own hearts, we have failed to take account of what God is calling us to do and the priorities that he is inviting us to set. And it is not just the things that we have actually done that amount to a breach of God's ways; it's the things that we have 'left undone' as well.

The last short sentence in the first part of the Confession comes with a heavy blow: 'There is no health in us.' Some English words have changed their meaning over the centuries, and the word 'health' is one of them. This prayer was written in the 1500s, when 'health' didn't just mean physical wellbeing. Nor did it mean 'mental health', in the modern scientific sense. It meant wholeness, being sound. If we translate this into modern language, then, 'there is no health in us' means that we are broken and unsound: in moral terms, we, like the rest of humanity, are in crisis. In short, we need God. That realization is what really matters, and without it nothing is gained by listing wrong things done or good things not done.

Restoration

So far the Confession has taken us to rock-bottom. It's the next part of the prayer that starts to lift us up again:

But thou, O Lord, have mercy upon us, miserable offenders.

> Spare thou them, O God, which confess their faults. Restore thou them that are penitent; according to thy promises declared unto mankind in Christ Jesu our Lord.

We've got to the place which our friend remembered: the place where we tell God that we are miserable. Thankfully, here is another case of a word shifting its meaning significantly. Nowadays, the word means sad or gloomy, but in the 1500s it had the meaning of 'needing to be pitied, needing mercy'. So 'miserable' here is a key word, because it looks forward to what the rest of the confession is going to pray for: the mercy and forgiveness of God. We are praying that God will spare and restore us. This is the point where we need to remember that a confession isn't quite the same thing as an apology, even if (as in some other Confessions) we use the word 'sorry'. We are praying for a fresh start, confident that God will give us what we are asking for: and that is what he promises 'in Christ'. This is an echo of Ephesians 4.32, 'be kind to one another, tender-hearted, forgiving one another, as God *in Christ* has forgiven you'. The point is that 'in Christ' there is the possibility of humankind's separation and alienation from God being healed (a topic that we will look at again in Chapter 14).

So our response to this is a determination to live a life that is really changed:

> And grant, O most merciful Father, for his sake, that we may hereafter live a godly, righteous, and sober life, to the glory of thy holy Name.

In other words, we pray that our whole future manner of life will itself give glory to God, and that our lives will be 'sober' (that is, serious and responsible). We are to think of ourselves as stewards and trustees of each day of our lives, together with the opportunities it brings. And it is through the invitation to be Christlike, in a strong sense and without any sense of woolly sentimentality, that we ourselves are called to forgive others. It's not that the wrongs done to us don't matter – they may well matter a lot – but taking it to heart that a fresh start is both possible and necessary is the only way not to be shackled to the past.

Against God and neighbour

It might seem strange that this particular form of Confession doesn't include anything explicitly about doing wrong against other people. In the terms of this prayer (and in the Confession in the Prayer Book Communion service too), sin is something we have committed against God. If we are used to the *Common Worship* confession, 'we have sinned against [God] *and against our neighbour* in thought and word and deed', we might really think it odd that there is no mention in the Prayer Book of sinning against our neighbour. Why is this, especially since the New Testament takes sinning against another person very seriously (Matt. 18.21, for example)?

The answer is that when we sin against our neighbour – when we fail to act with Christlike love towards other human beings, and when we fail to take the leap of imaginative love that the gospel demands – we are in fact falling short of our duty towards God. So, far from failing to take any notice of 'sins against our neighbour', the Prayer Book Confession is in fact taking them more seriously, and again it's a matter for real confession and not just apology. There is nothing, and no place, from which God can be excluded, and that includes human relationships and inter-actions. If we sin against our neighbour, we are actually sinning against God. There is an echo here of the great judgement scene in Matthew's Gospel, where those whose sin was to fail to care for other people are told 'just as you did not do it to one of the least of these, you did not do it to me' (Matt. 25.45).

Guilt

At the beginning of the chapter we mentioned *guilt*. There are different kinds of guilt: one kind is truly unhealthy, and psychology shows us how destructive to a person clinging, unresolved guilt can be. That kind of guilt is capable of turning into self-hatred and being linked to issues of mental health, and when that appears it needs to be addressed in a proper professional therapeutic (healing) setting. But we also use the word guilt in a different way, within a religious context. Then it means the effect of our sin, often coupled with the *awareness* of our sin. That kind of guilt can be a spur to confession, and it is not necessarily unhealthy. But it is vital that we don't let guilt fester, either in ourselves or others. This is a similar point to the one we were looking at when we thought about the word 'miserable'. Miserable means 'needing to be pitied', but behind that meaning is the guarantee that God will pity us. Similarly, the Confession puts us in the place of lost sheep, only because lost sheep can be found and Jesus is our good shepherd. So it's essential that whenever we talk about guilt we also talk about being forgiven and restored. Faith shows us that sin is serious, damaging and destructive: but it's a very different thing, and a terrible travesty, to picture Christianity as loading a crushing burden of anxiety and guilt on people, and it's important that we don't slip into thinking or acting as if it does. The gospel, the good news of Jesus, isn't about making people feel hopeless or worthless, with no way out.

Absolution

In the words of the Confession we acknowledge our failure before God, and we ask to start again. The Confession itself isn't the whole story. Every confession is followed by an absolution: we are assured that God forgives. The one that is paired in the Prayer Book with this Confession declares that God 'pardoneth and absolveth all them that truly repent and unfeignedly believe his holy gospel'. Absolutions (like confessions) do more than look back to sins committed in the past. They look forward to the future. That helps to make sense of saying confessions, and

31

receiving absolutions, time after time. It is not as if every week (say) we get a top-up of grace and see the 'tank run empty' until the next service. Yes, there *may* be occasions when we do especially sense a burden of sin, perhaps from something particular that has touched our conscience recently, and we feel very sharply that we 'need putting right'. But there are other ways of looking at this repetition, this cycle, of confession and absolution. It witnesses to God's love. Provided we are sincere, and don't treat confession and absolution casually, then we can welcome them as a constant reassurance of God's readiness to rebuild us: 'If we say that we have no sin, we deceive ourselves, and the truth is not in us: but if we confess our sins, [God] is faithful and just to forgive us our sins, and to cleanse us from all unrighteousness' (1 John 1.8–9).

This whole aspect of the relationship between God and humankind is sometimes called *penitence*. We might say a confession at specific times in church services, but penitence exists all the time because it is a creative part of the bond between God and the people he loves. We could say then that we live with penitence, or that we live *in* penitence. Again let's make it clear that that does not mean play acting or driving ourselves down into an unhealthy cringing self-imposed sense of inadequacy. Rather, it is to live all the time with the possibility of a God-given change of direction, and the knowledge that we are of infinite worth to him.

To think about further

Do you truly feel restored and forgiven when you have made a confession and received absolution? If not, what do you sense is still needed?

Part 2: Believing

5

Why we have creeds and say them

We believe

Most traditional Sunday church services include a long declaration of faith called a creed, said by everyone together. It's very much part of the 'set pattern' of morning or evening prayer, as well as Holy Communion. People who have been coming to church services for years will have repeated those words hundreds, even thousands of times. But, apart from the fact that the book and the minister tell us to, why do we say the creeds? And why have we got them anyway?

One reason for thinking about these questions is that it would be strange to say a text (and certainly to *repeat* a text) if we weren't sure of the rationale for it. Another is that there are some religious bodies, including a number that describe themselves as honouring and respecting Jesus, that say it's a virtue *not* to have creeds. So for those of us who *do* have creeds, it makes sense to think why we have them, and why we say these particular words in our services.

So in this chapter and the next two, we shall look at this aspect of Christian belief. There are many books and articles that tell the detailed history of how the creeds came into being. In a few pages now, we can only scratch the surface, but perhaps that scratch will help to make sense of the whole business of saying creeds, and explain why the creeds (and one of them in particular, the so-called Nicene Creed) includes the statements that it does. Rather than plunge straight into the text of the creeds, we shall start one stage back: why did the Christian Church come to the view that statements of faith were worth having anyway? In the next chapter, we shall concentrate on the words of the Nicene

Creed about God the Father and Jesus Christ. And in the chapter after that, we shall think about the Holy Spirit, and what it means to use words such as 'Three in One' and 'Trinity' about God.

Describing God in the Hebrew tradition

If we go back to the Hebrew Scriptures (the Old Testament), there really isn't anything that corresponds to a creed. There is of course the statement which we've mentioned before, in Deuteronomy 6.4, which is called the *Shema* from its first word in Hebrew. Translated literally word-for-word, it reads: 'Hear, Israel: The Lord our God, the Lord, one.' If you look in English Bibles you'll see how the translators have expanded those few words to make a sentence that 'works' in English, but that involves adding extra words to what is in the sparse Hebrew text. There are some other passages that describe God or make statement about him: for example, the mysterious name which could mean 'I am who I am' or 'I will be what I will be' (Ex. 3.14). And again, it is virtually a title for God that he is 'the Lord who brought the people of Israel up out of the land of Egypt' and who will bring them back from exile (Jer. 26.7-8). God is described in many word-pictures, including the skilful potter (Isa. 64.8) and the loving husband (Hos. 2.16). But there is nothing quite like a creed in the Hebrew Scriptures. God is described in action, story and poetry, not in statements. And that's the way of thinking that the early Christian Church inherited.

Beginning to describe belief about Jesus, crucified and risen

Christianity is first and foremost an encounter with Jesus of Nazareth. It is a faith centred on a person, not on ideas, concepts or words. The reason why Christian writings first came into being was to draw people into a relationship with God through Jesus Christ, and for that to be grounded in truth.

The New Testament writings set out to do this. The authors were writing in the aftermath of a unique event: the resurrection of Jesus. From the first days, the distinctiveness of the Christian faith rests on the claim that Jesus died on the day we call Good Friday; and that then, on the third day following his death, that is on the first Easter Day, his tomb was found empty. He had been raised to new life: not resuscitated (like someone whose heart had stopped but had begun beating again) nor woken out of a coma to carry on with life as before, nor vanished, but risen. The New Testament tells that a number of Jesus' followers met and saw him after he had risen, until, after some time, he parted from them: and after that event, which we call the Ascension, they did not meet and see him any more in that way.

Belief in resurrection was not new. Many Jews (including the group called the Pharisees whom we meet in the Gospels) already believed that the time would come when God would raise the dead bodily. But there was something distinctive about the faith that grew up around belief in Jesus' resurrection, and which became identifiable as the Christian faith, distinct from Judaism. First, Jesus' followers believed that he had a unique part in God's scheme, because he overcame death and was the first to rise. He alone had experienced resurrection, the pioneer of the resurrection of all the dead which still lay in the future: this is the point made in passages such as 1 Corinthians 15.20 and Galatians 1.18. Second, his death on Good Friday was far more than a criminal's execution, much more even than a martyr's death, and more than a demonstration of his love: Jesus' followers believed that his was a 'saving death', that is, it had the effect of changing the relationship between God and the whole of humanity. (We shall look at this subject more closely in Chapter 14.)

The Gospels are weighted heavily towards the events that took place around the time of Jesus' death and resurrection, but of course they also tell of his ministry beforehand. We read about Jesus as a teacher, a friend of people on the margins of respectable society, and a critic of the misuse of religious authority: think of the parable of the Pharisee and tax-collector praying in the temple

(Luke 18.9–14) which echoes all three of those themes. Yes, there are aspects of Jesus' ministry that are remarkable while not being unique, in that it would have been possible for another gifted and courageous spiritual person to do and say much the same kind of thing. But the style of the Gospels is not to have flat diary entries about Jesus teaching and preaching. Crucially, the Gospel authors were writing about events before Jesus' resurrection, but from the viewpoint of some years after it. So we find them weaving together different strands of thinking, many of them definitively linked to the resurrection and the belief that Jesus was unique.

That was not solely a matter of Jesus having said and done things, or for things to have happened to him, that his followers could not remember happening to anyone else. This goes to a different level: there was something about Jesus that marked him out from other human beings, not only in the depth of his love for people, not only in the brilliance of his teaching, or the strength of his dedication to God. It was not a matter of the extent to which he did things that other people could, possibly, have done. Those followers believed that Jesus was, in his nature and being, both the *same* as other people and also *different* from other people. The Gospel writers' conviction that Jesus, crucified and risen, had a unique place in God's plan for humanity is shown in the way that they wrote their accounts of his earthly ministry. That doesn't mean that they wrote a fantasy about Jesus' ministry, but at the same time they were not setting out to write a journal. They were writing gospel, 'good news' (in Greek, *euangelion*). Their job was to explain and convince.

'Christ' and 'Messiah'

The first Christians realized that Jesus had a significance that extended to the whole of humanity. They saw Jesus as the 'anointed one' (in Hebrew 'Messiah' and in Greek 'Christ'). The stage when Peter says to Jesus, 'You are the Christ' (Mark 8.29) is one of the pivotal moments of the Gospel.

The background is that many Jews believed that God would send at least one Messiah: a ruler, champion or royal figure. Jesus did not fit everybody's previous expectation of what that Anointed One would be like and what he would do: for example, many expected that the Messiah would be a military leader (perhaps that lies behind the episode where the people tried to make Jesus king, John 6.15). But insofar as Jesus did not fit any such expectations, the message of the Gospels is that God has shown how the concept of Messiah has to be reshaped in the light of what had actually happened through the person of Jesus. John writes that the whole of the Gospel is written so that we might believe that Jesus is the Messiah (John 20.31): we might add, Messiah in the true and authentic sense.

The servant of God

Those early followers who recognized Jesus' uniqueness thought about the passages in the Old Testament that paint a picture of a person who has a special role in relation to God and humanity. They saw links and parallels between those passages and what they knew and understood about Jesus. They read the parts of the book of Isaiah about the suffering servant of God (chapters 42 and 49–53). They recalled the part of the book of Daniel (7.9–14) that tells of coming judgement and of 'one like a human being' who is presented to God to be given power and kingship. They believed that many other ideas and concepts, especially those from the Scriptures, were connected to one focal point, which they saw in terms of Jesus himself. They came to use the titles Son of God (Mark 1.1) and Son of Man (Mark 14.41; John 3.13) distinctively of Jesus.[3]

The New Testament is evidence of the energy and dynamism with which the early Christians strove (as we might say, under God's guidance) to understand God's mission to the world

---

3 The titles that the New Testament writers used for Jesus is a huge subject in itself. For instance, in Hebrew, 'son of x' does not necessarily have any biological meaning, but can denote a characteristic. It really does seem likely that Jesus used the title 'Son of Man' (which is how God addresses the prophet Ezekiel) for himself.

through Jesus. When we read it, we have to remember that they were exploring and sifting ideas in the aftermath of an event which they knew was world-changing and had massive significance for the whole of human history, but which had only happened a very few years before the earliest books were written. The writers of the New Testament used different methods to show what they believed about Jesus: statements about him in relation to the whole of creation (such as John 1.1–14 and Col. 1.15–16), and picture language and vision (such as Rev. 1.12–18). Paul's letters are full of his worked-out conclusions about Jesus. In addition to all this, the Gospels are carefully written to show that throughout his work of teaching, caring and healing he had more than 'ordinary' authority. Often this is done by picking up themes and images from the Old Testament. We find this in passages such as Mark 1.21–2.12, in the Transfiguration where Jesus is revealed in divine glory (Mark 9.2–8), Matthew's 'set piece' when Jesus delivers a new law on a mountain (Matt. 5–7), and his triumphal entry into Jerusalem (Mark 11.8–10).

Is Jesus really unique?

All of the New Testament was written from a position that, first, God had acted uniquely through Jesus, and, second, Jesus was personally unique and not simply a specially gifted or favoured man. Mainstream Christianity has always agreed on those two points. There have, however, always been people who have found the first of these points easier to accept than the second. They would say that Jesus was a gifted teacher and healer who annoyed the authorities to the point of being condemned; for whatever reason, a story that he was more than a human being was invented around him. On that basis, they say, it ought to be possible to wash away all the extra material and be left with an account of the 'real man' without any of the supposed invented additions that fill the pages of the New Testament. However, that line of argument is to misunderstand both the experience of the disciples and the process by which the New Testament was written. It is true that most New Testament scholars are at least open to the possibility that some scenes in the Gospels are composed in order to convey a truth about Jesus, and that that underlying truth is more important than the question whether the scene is an absolute literal record. But that is very far from saying that the Gospels are fiction, wrapping up a legend in a historical setting.

The mainstream Christian position is this: belief about Jesus is something that God has given and made possible, and it is not something that has been made up. In other words, the Church's claim is that what it believes about Jesus and his resurrection is *a real and actual truth that God has revealed* and not *something that people have invented* – not even something that was invented from good motives, to try and explain the experience that the disciples had.

Putting Christian belief into ordered words

The New Testament writers tell about Jesus in many different ways, and none of them tries to set out a single statement of everything there is to say about Jesus. The Bible writers of the first Christian decades did not set out to write anything like the creeds we use in church services. There are, however, some parts of the New Testament that look as if they might quote from short declarations of Christian belief. Perhaps texts of that kind would have been learned by heart, and repeated by the first Christians. One such text could simply be 'Jesus is Lord!' (1 Cor. 12.3). The best-known longer passage of this kind is Philippians 2.5–11, which tells of Christ being obedient to the point of death and then being exalted by God, and another is 1 Timothy 3.16, which we shall look at in our closing chapter.

Discerning the truth about Jesus

From very early on, there were different ideas about Jesus in circulation. Christians recognized the importance of sifting what is true from what is not (we use a word borrowed from Greek, orthodox, to mean right-believing). Otherwise it would be impossible for the Church to hold together around a core of dependable truth. We know that in early times there were differences of opinion within individual Christian communities (1 Cor. 1), a fear of unsound ideas supplanting what was authentic (2 Tim. 4.3), and groups that held views contrary to others (Rev. 2.15). But Christians believed that, if truth comes from God, it is the Church's job to pray and to think carefully, and so to discern what the actual truth is. Putting that into effect was a long and difficult task. It was some time before the contents of the New Testament (a 'canon') were fixed, so it does not fit the circumstances of those times to speak of being able to appeal to a body of authoritative and universally accepted Christian Scripture. And, second, even those books which did come to form the New Testament do not answer every question, or close off debate, about Jesus' identity and his relationship to the Father and the Spirit. And in addition to this, there were other religions in circulation at the time, and there was always the possibility of authentic Christian belief being confused with ideas that came from them.

And so, as time went on, let us say over the next three hundred years or so, the need was felt for some joined-up statements of belief in a style other than those brief declarations found in the New Testament. That need was greatest when there was a major dispute or a serious uncertainty to settle. Arguments were passionate and sometimes bitter. It wouldn't be right to imagine that debate was banned, or that everyone even within the compass of 'orthodox' Christianity had to hold the same views about everything.[4] But it came to be recognized that there had to be limits, and there were ideas that were so seriously adrift from or-

---

4 The word *adiaphora* is used for matters which may be significant and give rise to passionate disagreement, but are not fundamental issues of faith over which the Church must divide. For an instance where Paul deals with a question on these lines, see 1 Cor. 10.23–33; see also Acts 15. It is still a live issue today, in a Church that encompasses different views on teaching and order, how to discern those areas which can be regarded as *adiaphora* and those which cannot.

thodox teaching that they threatened the viability and rationale of Christianity. And to those ideas the word 'heresy' (from a word meaning 'faction') came to be applied.

To cut a long story very short, creeds were invented to do a number of things. They express the Church's officially agreed corporate belief: a statement of agreed doctrine. They were a declaration of faith that people would personally assent to, typically when they were baptized. They could be used in worship when a congregation corporately affirms its belief. And they could be used as a means of identifying who was orthodox, because the people who had unorthodox beliefs – heretics – would not be able in conscience to say the words of the creed, especially if the creed contains statements that were specifically written to safeguard the orthodox position. Through the course of Christian history, the texts we call creeds have done all these things.

Centred on Jesus

As far as their content is concerned, it is no surprise that Christian creeds usually have a lot to say about Jesus, because the story of how and why we have creeds began with questions about him. The early Christians' experience of Jesus, and the thinking that they did about him, had an influence on how they pictured God, and the belief that came to be about the Holy Spirit. So if it had not been for the Church taking on the task of discerning the truth about Jesus, there would be no such things as creeds. And in the next chapter we shall look further at what the creeds say about Jesus.

To think about further

Read some of the Bible passages listed in this chapter. What picture of Jesus and what impression of the New Testament writers emerge as you do that?

6

Belief about Jesus Christ

Of one Being with the Father

In the last chapter we touched on the reasons why the Church moved towards having statements of belief in an organized point-by-point form. It's from those early centuries that we get the two creeds that are used regularly in worship. One of them is the so-called Apostles' Creed, often used in morning and evening prayer. We don't know exactly when it was written, but it's possible to estimate that a version existed by about 200. It had reached substantially the form that we would recognize by about 340, and exactly the Latin text from which our English versions are translated by about 700. It was based on a text that converts were asked to say before they were baptized, and it was probably also used as a teaching aid. There is no historical basis for the old story that each of the twelve apostles contributed a phrase to the Apostles' Creed but, among the creeds in modern use, this is the one that most clearly and plainly reworks phrases from Scripture. To that extent it is most obviously rooted in the Christian thinking of early years and the words and thought forms that were in circulation in the time of the Apostles.

The other creed familiar to us is the one we customarily use at Holy Communion, and which is usually called the Nicene Creed. It was adopted at a summit meeting known as the First Council of Nicaea (325) and then again, in a revised version, at another meeting, the First Council of Constantinople in 381. With one important exception (about the Holy Spirit, which we shall look at in the next chapter), the text of the Creed as it is used today was settled then. The original text of the Creed as it came from the

Council is in the plural: 'We believe ...' because its purpose was to declare the Church's shared, corporate, orthodox belief: the belief that prevailed when other opinions about God and Jesus were rejected. It is written in the plural – 'we believe' – because it is in effect the communiqué of a major international meeting, recording the conclusion that the participants agreed.

Corporate belief

To say 'the Church's agreed and officially approved belief is as follows' is different from saying 'as a group of individual Christians we think this'. The Nicene Creed is the declaration of the Church as a body, using the full weight of its authority, at a time when different teachings were in circulation. There was a real concern that disunity of belief was damaging, and that wrong teaching was actually dangerous. So when congregations in churches today begin the Creed with the words 'We believe', as distinct from 'I believe', we are not downplaying the importance of personal faith, but we are saying that faith is not *solely* a matter of individual assent or commitment. We are declaring the shared faith of the Church, not simply affirming that we personally believe it.[5]

Here then is the beginning of the Nicene Creed:

We believe in one God, the Father, the Almighty, maker of heaven and earth, of all that is, seen and unseen.

We believe in one Lord, Jesus Christ, the only Son of God, eternally begotten of the Father, God from God, Light from Light, true God from true God, begotten, not made, of one Being with the Father; through him all things were made.

For us and for our salvation he came down from heaven, was incarnate from the Holy Spirit and the Virgin Mary and

---

5 The form 'I believe' eventually took the place of 'We believe' in the context of worship, and when the fact that the Creed had been produced as the *corporate* statement of a council was no longer the principal.

was made man. For our sake he was crucified under Pontius Pilate; he suffered death and was buried. On the third day he rose again in accordance with the Scriptures; he ascended into heaven and is seated at the right hand of the Father. He will come again in glory to judge the living and the dead, and his kingdom will have no end.

The first thing that strikes us is how brief the Creed's statement about God the Father is, and how much more it says about Jesus Christ. This fits in with the points we were thinking about in the previous chapter. The creeds are concerned with stating and safeguarding orthodox belief about Jesus. It was important that the Church set out correct teaching about who Jesus *is*, for the sake of understanding what he *does*. Christians believe that what Jesus Christ does is to bring *salvation*, and the Creed sets out points that are essential for that belief.

Salvation

Salvation is a very 'religious-sounding' word. Like most religious words, if we go back far enough, we come to a time when everyday words were used for religious ideas, rather than religion having a set of words of its own. Salvation is a concept that goes back to the Old Testament, and which hinges on the ordinary word for rescue (*yasha'*). In essence, the idea of salvation is simply this: God rescues his people. So, for instance, the Jewish people have always looked far, far back into the past, to the time when God brought Moses and their ancestors out of Egypt, as a time of rescue. The triumph song in Exodus 15 includes these words: 'The Lord is my strength and my might, and he has become my salvation [or rescue]' (Ex. 15.2). The initial meaning of salvation or rescue is very immediate and applies to everyday life. In that ancient setting, the kind of things that the people are rescued from are physical danger, or oppression and death at the hands of their enemies. Salvation brings peace, freedom and security.

By the time we come to the New Testament, the meaning of salvation has changed and developed. It means being saved from sin and its effects, including separation and alienation from God. And since from Old Testament times death has been seen as a consequence of sin (Gen. 2.17; compare Rom. 5.12 and 6.23), so salvation is now understood in terms of rescue from death, or from being destroyed or punished for ever. The New Testament sets out to show how Jesus brings this rescue about: 'God has destined us not for wrath but for obtaining salvation through our Lord Jesus Christ, who died for us' (1 Thess. 5.9–10). So, in the thinking of the New Testament, the salvation that Jesus achieves is of ultimate, everlasting significance. There have been different ways of understanding *how* he does this (see Chapter 14), but it has always been central to Christian belief *that* he does. The creeds are the testimony of the Christians of the first centuries, as they worked to express the Church's understanding about Jesus, and how it was that he makes salvation available to humanity.

Human and divine

By the time the need for creeds arose, the content or 'canon' of the New Testament was well on the way to becoming settled, which set the context for the work of the thinkers who were working at that time. They realized that inherent in the Christian Scriptures were two guiding principles. Put briefly, one is that Jesus can only bring salvation if he is fully *identified* with humanity. The other is that he can only bring salvation if he has the necessary divine *power*. Already in the New Testament we can see how this idea was being articulated and put into words: Paul makes a striking 'both-and' statement about Jesus when he says that as God's Son he 'was descended from David according to the flesh' and also 'was declared to be Son of God with power according to the spirit of holiness by resurrection from the dead' (Rom. 1.3–4).

That twofold statement has implications which are fundamentally important. First, the New Testament writers insisted that

Jesus Christ shared humanity in common with all other people. That is because what happened to Jesus – his resurrection – shows God's plan for all humanity: he is the 'first fruits of those who have died' (1 Cor. 15.20, 23). Jesus is unique *so far*, in that he is the only person to experience resurrection: but in God's time, humanity at large will share it. Furthermore, if Jesus were not human, and *fully* human, or if he were some sort of spirit-being who only appeared to be human, then his resurrection would have nothing to do with the rest of humankind. It might be a demonstration of power, but it would not be a promise to the whole of humanity. Paul explains this principle by reference to the figure of Adam. *Adam* is the Hebrew for human being. Adam stands for humankind, of which (as Genesis tells) he is the first member. In Paul's language (and whether Adam was a historical or mythical figure, his point still holds) Christ is the second Adam, and undoes the damage of Adam's disobedience (Rom. 5.14); 'as all die in Adam, so all will be made alive in Christ' (1 Cor. 15.22). Jesus Christ is the representative of renewed humanity, from inside the human race and not from outside it. A similar point is made by the unnamed writer of the letter to the Hebrews, who writes that Christ

> had to become like his brothers [i.e. fellow human beings] in every respect, so that he might be a merciful and faithful high priest ... Because he himself was tested by what he suffered, he is able to help those who are being tested ... we do not have a high priest who is unable to sympathize with our weaknesses, but we have one who in every respect has been tested as we are, yet without sin. (Heb. 2.17–18; 4.15)

And second, alongside this, there is a strong New Testament theme of Jesus having divine authority and power: it comes in the opening chapters of John, Colossians, Hebrews and Revelation, for example, and in the closing scene of Matthew's Gospel. In the 'creed-writing period' of the 300s, orthodox thinkers likewise insisted that it is not enough to think of Jesus as being an especially good or spiritual man, or a specially empowered representative of God – even if there never had been such a great representative of God before, and never would be again.[6]

Christianity among the religions

The scene is set for the Church to work towards putting into words the classic Christian belief about Jesus Christ, both human and divine. It was not only a matter of Christian belief being defined in contrast to the inherited assumptions of the Jewish faith – namely, that God is God, and everything else is absolutely *not* God. There was also a need to distinguish Christianity from a range of other religions that were in circulation in the ancient world. That included a host of other beliefs and myths which told of angels, demons, gods and hybrid beings that were part god and part human. Myths about gods and heroes had been part of Greek and Roman literature for centuries; there were also some legends and visionary writings on what we might call the fringe of Judaism.

Equally a cause of concern were religious groups (called Gnostics, pronounced *noss*-tix) that held the belief that there was a body of secret knowledge about gods and supernatural beings which only people initiated into the religion were allowed to learn. That so-called 'knowledge' (in Greek *gnōsis*) sometimes included ideas borrowed from Judaism and early Christianity, and it seems that Christian leaders were worried that the Gnostics might divert people from real faith by falsely claiming to know more about Jesus than the apostles and those in their circle did. This was a long-standing problem: a number of New Testament passages seem to warn against paying heed to Gnostic teaching (for

---

6 Believing that Christ is divine does not mean that we understand everything about what that means, and (for example) we do not have to take it as implying that he held an infinite amount of knowledge about the whole universe in his mind at every moment from his conception and birth onwards. Belief about Jesus' divinity does not stand or fall on that question.

example, 1 Tim. 1.3–5 and 2 Cor. 11.4) and Paul ends 1 Timothy
with a warning to '[a]void the profane chatter and contradictions
of what is falsely called knowledge; by professing it some have
missed the mark as regards the faith' (1 Tim. 6.20–21). It was vital
for the early Church to avoid confusion between authentic faith
and other versions; and to ensure that Jesus was not portrayed as
just another of the legendary and mythical figures that appeared
in the legends told by the Gnostics and others.

Challenges to orthodox belief

Orthodox Christianity needed to hold its ground against a
number of ways of describing or understanding Jesus that were
beyond what could be accommodated within its limits – the
heresies. Again, it may be useful to outline some of the characteristics of the heresies, because that gives us a background against
which we can understand why the Creed says what it does.

In a nutshell, the supporters of the heresies were the people who
found it impossible to accept that Jesus was both fully divine and
fully human. So their solution was to say that he was one or the
other, but not both. Some people went in the direction of saying
that he was only human: maybe he was divinely inspired and a
very special man, they said, but not divine. A variation on this idea
was to say that Jesus was adopted as God's Son when he was born
or baptized (when a voice came from heaven proclaiming that he
was God's Son, Mark 1.11), but that was a change that took place
at a definite point of history and therefore Jesus had not been the
Son of God from before time began. Other people went in the
opposite direction: Jesus was not a real human at all, but a spirit-
being of some sort who only had the *appearance* of being human.
So, they said, there was no 'incarnation' – becoming flesh –
because, whoever and whatever Jesus was, he was never fully
human. He had not really and truly become flesh.

Another way of 'squaring the circle' that gained quite a lot of
currency was to put forward a compromise, to think of Jesus as

divine and partly (but not fully) human, or human and partly (but not fully) divine. Some people thought that Jesus was in some way or to some extent divine *but* that he had been created by God: he had been 'made'. A rather subtle version of this was to say that before time began God planned that the Son would come into existence, but that plan was not put into effect until Jesus was born: in other words Christ had not *actually* existed from eternity. So, supporters of that idea said that the plan was eternal, but Christ was not; and they made something of a slogan out of the key sentence of their argument, '*there was a time when he did not exist*'. Consequently, they said, the Son and the Father did not fully share the same essence of being God: the Son's being was *like* the Father's but was not the *same*. This belief was called Arianism. It was perhaps the most persistent and widely followed of the teachings that were finally rejected as 'heretical', and there were periods when it had the support of the most powerful people in the empire.

Added to that, there were other beliefs that were rejected by the mainstream Church. They included the suggestion that the Old Testament was worthless and that the God who appears in it was not the same as the heavenly Father of Jesus. Consequently, they claimed, 'God the Father Almighty' was not the 'maker of heaven and earth, and of all that is, seen and unseen'. There are more rejected teachings and variations than this, but for the time being that list of different ideas is long and complicated enough.

Why the Creed says what it does

So there was what we might call a busy religious market-place. If we put together the points we have already looked at, plus other truths that the Church was concerned to maintain, the 'headlines' of the beliefs that had to be set out strongly were these: that there was one God; that Jesus Christ was fully divine and fully human and that he, and he alone, brings salvation to humanity; and that the Holy Spirit too was fully divine (a topic we shall look at more closely in the next chapter). There was to be no room given to an idea of Jesus or the Spirit being a kind of second-rank god, or a god-like being that did not have all the powers and characteristics that God has. At the same time, it was important to find a way of describing the relationship between God the Father, Jesus Christ and the Holy Spirit, that was compatible with Gospel passages that show Jesus praying to the Father (crucially in the Garden of Gethsemane before his arrest, Mark 14.32–36); and the account in John's Gospel of Jesus telling the disciples that he will ask the Father to send the Holy Spirit to them (John 14.15–17, 26).

It ought then to become clear how, and why, the Nicene Creed is designed to guard against opinions and teachings that did not match the ones that the Church finally adopted as being true. If we look again at the heresies as we have described them, we can match them to lines in the Nicene Creed which state the orthodox teaching instead. So then, the Creed teaches that there is one God (not many). He, and not some other second-rank god, did make everything seen and unseen. In order to counter the teachings of the Arians, the Creed describes Jesus Christ as 'Lord' – a divine title. It stresses that he has existence and sonship from eternity, that is, he was begotten and not created. He shares the same essence of being with the Father, 'true God from true God'. He 'came down from heaven' – that is, he was not an earthly mortal adopted by God; 'for us and for our salvation' – in other words, our salvation and our ultimate destiny depend on his coming into the world, and on his death and resurrection. 'Incarnate from the Holy Spirit and the Virgin Mary' puts together in one phrase the record of Matthew's and Luke's Gospels about the birth of Jesus, and it mirrors the bold statement in John's Gospel which Gnostics could not accept, that 'the Word became flesh and lived among us' (Matt. 1.18; Luke 1.26–35; John 1.14).

The Creed insists that the death and resurrection of Jesus are historic events. 'In accordance with the Scriptures' is a phrase borrowed from 1 Corinthians 15.3–4 where Paul writes about Jesus' dying and rising as being an inevitable consequence of what God has revealed, according to the message of the Scriptures – by which he meant the Old Testament taken together (a point made also in Luke 24.26). And the themes of glory, judgement and eternal rule also come directly from the New Testament (for example, Matt. 25.31 and Rev. 5.13; 11.15).

So each line or 'clause' in the Creed safeguards a particular belief that the greatest thinkers of the early centuries came to realize was essential to Christianity. In the terms that they wrote, the creeds do not have any optional extras. Take any of the statements in the creeds away, and we can as it were hear the voice of our forebears warning us that we are removing an aspect of faith that is vital to a true understanding of God and Jesus Christ.

The Nicene Creed doesn't claim to say everything that can be said about Jesus, and we have seen how the words, ideas and concepts in it tell us a lot about the kind of controversies and questions that concerned the Church in the age when it was written. Times have moved on, and some of the heresies have faded into the background of history,[7] but it is still vital for Christians to think about, and (as far as we can) understand, Jesus Christ and his place in God's gift of salvation. When we say this Creed, we are walking in the footsteps of the people who struggled with the terms of belief, and who worked hard on behalf of the Church to find a form of words that could witness truly to God's being and to what he has done through Jesus.

To think about further

Here are some words from another declaration of faith from the early Church, called the Athanasian Creed.[8]

> We believe and declare that our Lord Jesus Christ, the Son of God, is both divine and human.

---

7 But for an interesting exploration of some modern implications of historic heresies, see Ben Quash and Michael Ward (eds), 2007, *Heresies and How to Avoid Them*, London: SPCK.
8 This version is part of the Affirmation of Faith (E7) in *New Patterns for Worship*.

God, of the being of the Father, the only Son from before time began; human from the being of his mother, born in the world; fully God and fully human; human in both mind and body.

As God he is equal to the Father, as human he is less than the Father.

Although he is both divine and human he is not two beings but one Christ.

One, not by turning God into flesh, but by taking humanity into God; truly one, not by mixing humanity with Godhead, but by being one person.

For as mind and body form one human being so the one Christ is both divine and human.

How helpful do you find the languages of the creeds in expressing the uniqueness of Jesus?

What other words might you use?

7

Believing in the Holy Spirit and the Trinity

The Spirit, worshipped and glorified

In the last section of the Nicene Creed, we find these lines that refer to the Holy Spirit:

> We believe in the Holy Spirit, the Lord, the giver of life, who proceeds from the Father and the Son, who with the Father and the Son is worshipped and glorified, who has spoken through the prophets.

The word we translate 'spirit' – *pneuma* in Greek – is the ordinary word for breath, wind or air, like the equivalent Hebrew word, *ruah* (with a hard *h*). From the outset we should not assume that Old Testament would have intended *ruah* to mean 'the Holy Spirit' in the full Christian sense. Prime examples where we should not make assumptions of that kind would be the phrases 'holy spirit' and 'spirit of God' (for example, Ps. 51.11 and Gen. 1.2).

The Spirit in the New Testament

But in the New Testament we see a move in the direction of the word 'spirit' being used to mean a distinct dynamic force, which actually *is* the presence of God. The writers of the New Testament show the Spirit being active in God's plan for humanity: they understood that the Spirit was at work in the writings of the Old Testament (Heb. 10.15) and in the birth of Jesus (chiefly at Luke

1.35, the message of the angel to Mary, but also in many other places in Luke's opening chapters). The Spirit appears at Jesus' baptism (Mark 1.10) and is present in Jesus' ministry: Luke, for whom the Spirit is a central theme, shows Jesus 'filled with the power of the Spirit' opening his ministry by applying the words of Isaiah 61 to himself, 'The Spirit of the Lord is upon me' (Luke 4.14–21). At the end of his Gospel, Luke records the risen Jesus ordering the apostles to wait in Jerusalem until they 'have been clothed with power from on high' (Luke 24.49). That promise is fulfilled after Jesus' ascension, the last of the appearances he makes after his resurrection, and the Spirit comes on the apostles at Pentecost (Acts 2.14). John's Gospel gives essentially the same message in a different setting, as Jesus, before his death, promises his disciples that he will ask the Father to send 'the Advocate, the Holy Spirit, whom the Father will send in my name, [who] will teach you everything, and remind you of all that I have said to you' (John 14.26); and then, in one of the appearances after his resurrection, Jesus breathes on the disciples and tells them, 'Receive the Holy Spirit' (John 20.22).

After the ascension and Pentecost, the followers of Jesus experienced God's power present and active among them. It was not enough to think of the Holy Spirit as a 'thing' that is separate from God or that comes *from* God, like a message or signal. The Holy Spirit, they realized, is active in his own right. The strand of Christian thinking on these lines is also reflected in Mark's Gospel, where Jesus told his disciples that when they are called to give their testimony in times of persecution, 'it is not you who speak, but the Holy Spirit' (Mark 13.11). The Spirit proactively directs the work of the young Church and its representatives, even stopping Paul and Timothy from preaching in Asia Minor when their true calling is to go to Macedonia (Acts 16.6). In 2 Corinthians 3.17–18 Paul writes boldly: 'Now the Lord is the Spirit … [a]nd all of us … are being transformed … for this comes from the Lord, the Spirit.' Paul's use of words in that passage not only makes it clear that the Spirit is active but also gives the Spirit the divine title 'Lord'.

Being in the Spirit

The New Testament writers show the Spirit at work in the shared life of the Church, and also in individuals, including those who are new to the faith. Paul gives a picture of this in 1 Corinthians 12. Elsewhere too he explains how the Spirit inspires and transforms people: '[Y]ou are not in the flesh; you are in the Spirit, since the Spirit of God dwells in you' (Rom. 8.9). The Spirit is God-in-power, making it possible for people to live a life that is touched by the resurrection of Jesus, that is, a life marked by knowing that God has overcome death through Jesus: humanity is no longer in the grip of separation from God and all its negative effects, '[f]or the law of the Spirit of life in Christ Jesus has set you free from the law of sin and of death' (Rom. 8.2). In the same way, while resurrection for all still lies in God's future (2 Tim. 2.18), the effect of what God has done in Christ is available, here and now.

And so this life is to be lived in a new way. The old way of being (and therefore the old way of thinking and acting), which Paul calls the flesh, has been overtaken by the new way: life in the Spirit, life that recognizes God's promises and looks forward to their ultimate and complete fulfilment. Paul's use of the word 'flesh' in contrast to spirit does not mean that Christians should be disparaging about physical existence and bodies (a potential misunderstanding which is corrected in 1 Tim. 4.3). Nor does it mean that Christians should ignore the physical practicalities of daily life. In other words, being 'in the Spirit' does not mean withdrawing from life as we know it, but it means living in the light of a renewed understanding of God's plan for humankind. And the offer to which the New Testament witnesses is that being 'in the Spirit' is for everyone who believes that Jesus is the Christ of God. In Paul's language, 'you are in the Spirit' is a message to which all Christians must be able to hear and respond, and it is not only for particular 'spiritual specialists' or heroes. To 'be in the Spirit' is to be joined in this enterprise of new life, renewal and love in God's name: to hear this piece of good news that is at the heart of the Christian gospel, that is, that God in Christ has overcome death, and that God has made it possible for the relationship between himself and humanity, damaged by human sin and failure, to be restored.

Talking about the Spirit

The language that the New Testament uses about the Spirit is marked by a sense of reality, strength and presence. That's very different from the way that we sometimes use the words 'spirit' and 'spirituality'. When we think about the Holy Spirit, we need to put out of our minds any suggestion of something that is vague, wispy, weak, or a shadowy echo. 'Holy Spirit' carries the meaning of God active in power, not a remembrance of God absent, and certainly not a mere feeling that lacks any substance apart from our emotions. We might find it helpful to think of the range of English words that correspond to *pneuma*: the idea of 'God the holy wind' might be helpful because it suggests power and move-ment, and 'holy breath' suggests life.

As well as Holy Spirit, the New Testament writers used other terms for this energy and power of God that directs and drives the Church's work and mission. We have already looked at a place in the Gospel of John which uses the word *paraklētos* (borrowed into English as 'Paraclete'), which combines the concepts of comforter, advocate and strengthener. Luke, as we have seen, uses 'power' as a term for the promised Spirit at Pentecost.

The Spirit as Person

In the last chapter, we looked at the way in which the Church realized that it would not do to describe Christ as a lesser or limited god, or a second-rank, god-like being. The Church also understood that the same applied to the Spirit. It looked to passages which speak together of Father, Son and Spirit (Matt.

28.19) and Jesus Christ, God and the Spirit (2 Cor. 13.13). Acts 2.33 speaks of Christ at the right hand of God, receiving and then pouring out the Holy Spirit. The conclusion, which was definitively put into words as part of orthodox Christian teaching, is that the Spirit too is divine. When the Creed uses the words 'The Holy Spirit, the Lord', it ensures that the Holy Spirit is recognized as God, 'worshipped and glorified' with the Father and Son, and that he has been existing and active from before the ages. It affirms that the Spirit has spoken through the prophets: that is, the Old Testament was written under the guidance of the Spirit, and the Spirit did not begin to act only in Jesus' time.

Trinity

It was an important element in the Church's reflection on the divine nature of Father, Son and Spirit to see God existing in a relationship of perfect love, within his own being. So the Church's thinkers set out the teaching that God, while being One, is Trinity (the 'three-ness' of Father, Son and Spirit). It is important to say again that they understood their task to be to discern what God was revealing about himself, in other words that they were putting themselves under the guidance of the Holy Spirit to be able to say what was true. They did not believe that they were inventing anything by human power or ingenuity: it was a matter of truth, not speculation. As they looked for words to describe the relationship between the Father, Son and Spirit, they used language about parenthood rather than creation, and said that the Son had been 'eternally begotten' of the Father.[9] The word they used for the relationship between the Father and the Spirit reflects the dynamic described by Jesus in John 14.16–17, 'I will ask the Father, and he will give you another Advocate, to be with you

---

9 'Eternally begotten' in the Creed refers to the relationship of the Son to the Father before time began. It does not refer to the birth of Jesus from Mary, which happened at a particular time and place.

for ever. This is the Spirit of truth'. The form used to put that relationship in the Creed was to say that the Spirit 'proceeds'.

Belief, truth and experience

Some of the thinking and language in the debates and declarations of the early Christian centuries may seem to us to be abstract and theoretical. But the important principle for us to keep tight hold of is that they were rooted in prayer, God's revealing of himself, and the Church's experience. The Church's belief in the Trinity is the Church's understanding of how God is, based on how God has shown the truth about himself. The oneness of God is an essential principle in that belief, and nothing must detract from it – in other words, it was (and is) vital not to slip into a way of thinking that there were three gods. At the same time, it is important to honour the fact that God has revealed himself as three 'personal beings': Father, Son and Spirit.[10] Here again the Church's thinkers and leaders were cautious about possible mistakes. They said that it was wrong to think of God as a single being who simply presented himself in three ways (like an actor playing three roles): rather, the three-ness of God was something that was true of how he *is*, not just how he *appears*. The three Persons are distinct, but perfectly at one in love and purpose.

God's activity is the activity of the Trinity. God, Three and One, acts *together* in creation, in saving and rescuing humanity, in sustaining the life and work of the Church. But there are distinctions to maintain: for example, only the Son suffered and died on the cross; the Father and Spirit did not. Only the Spirit 'proceeds'; the Father and Son do not. But human language and thinking has its limits, and nobody suggests that by declaring the doctrine of the Trinity the Church has completely *understood* God.

---

10 The word Person is often used, but it does not mean that God consists of three *human*-type personalities. The word for personal being used by the Greek-speaking early Christian thinkers is *hypostasis*.

By describing the controversies as briefly as has been done here, we have scarcely done justice to the depth in which the questions were addressed those 1,700 years ago. But it is essential for us to bear this in mind: the conclusion of the mainstream Church was that any understanding of God, other than a fully Trinitarian doctrine, had some fatal flaw. None of the alternatives could be matched to an authentic and all-encompassing picture of God, his love and his work, without undermining a basic principle, or without risking injecting a terrible element of uncertainty into the question whether God really saves humanity.

Is right believing important?

The 300s were a critical phase in the history of the Church as it formulated its teaching. As we said earlier, when we recite the creeds, we are repeating words that inevitably bear the stamp of the questions that were uppermost in the fourth century. The writers of the creeds were reflecting on Scripture and experience, and trying to guard against misunderstandings and mistakes: they were not trying to make belief complicated. Mainstream Christianity (by which I mean all the major Christian denom- inations) has ever since kept to the teaching or doctrine of the Trinity of Father, Son and Spirit. And it would be in line with the traditional understanding held by the Trinitarian churches to suggest that the Spirit guided the Church towards real truth in formulating the Apostles' and Nicene Creeds.

Creeds were not originally invented in order to be said in weekly church services, but that has become part of our worshipping pattern. Using them in that way does have the positive effect that the classic formulas of the Christian faith, which were worked out so long ago, stay in the shared memory of the Church as a body. It also means that we witness to the fact that our forebears put such store on learning and teaching the truth about the Christian faith.

Critics may remark that disputes about religious belief have been mixed up with some very ugly episodes in history, from arguments conducted with pamphlets through discrimination to violence and persecution. Does that criticism discredit the whole principle that searching for religious truth is important? Others claim that religious statements of the kind the creeds contain only amount to speculation and guesswork. In the end (so the argument goes) we cannot know anything that we cannot prove by scientific means, so we should stop being so concerned about the search for religious truth. When that line of argument is taken to its limit it can take the form of suggesting that the quest for right belief is ultimately a waste of time. Words to do with truth and teaching such as 'doctrine' and 'dogma' have become uncomplimentary terms for hair-splitting, for an attitude that it is more important to be right than to be loving, and for stubborn unwillingness to change one's view in the face of contrary evidence.

Another way the argument sometimes goes is this: we have no way of knowing what is true about God or religious and spiritual things; so one person's idea is as valid as another's, and 'if you want to believe such-and-such, and it "works" for you, then that is fine'.

One of the reasons for having creeds, and keeping them, is to take another and very different approach to issues such as this. 'Classic' Christian belief maintains that although truths about God cannot be established in the same way that we can establish facts about (say) geography or mathematics, and while we must stay aware of our limitations and the possibility of being mistaken, nevertheless, there *are* such things as religious truths, and they *are*, actually, truths. It may be a different *kind* of truth to say that 'Jesus is the only-begotten Son of God', compared to other statements such as 'there are such things as electrons' or 'Paris is the capital of France': but theology, 'God-talk', claims *both* that such a statement about Jesus can be actually true *and* that it is important that the Church searches for the truth, and holds and teaches it. In societies such as those of modern western countries where people of different faiths live together, there has to be courtesy, sensitivity and humility in interfaith dialogue and contact, but at the same time it is quite legitimate for Christians to keep hold of the belief and principle that certain religious statements are true in an actual, objective sense. Living in a democratic society, where people are equally free to practise the religion of their choice, does not imply that one should think that all religions are equally true. And yes, 'acting right' must always stand alongside 'believing rightly' as elements of faith. Neither can be thrown overboard as being unimportant or not being essential to what living as a Christian entails.

Do we still need creeds?

Creeds might never have been needed if Jesus was a good and godly man, not divine in any sense, whose noble motives got him killed. If accounts of Jesus having risen are picture-language invented to symbolize the resilience of the human spirit, then the concept of the Trinity is nonsense and, again, we would have no use for creeds. And if nothing God had done in the past had any effect now, or if he was not active in power among his people, declarations of belief would be little more than historical curiosities. Christians of every age face the same questions as those which were addressed by our forebears of the early centuries. Has God really promised rescue? Did he overcome death in Jesus Christ? Is the Spirit active in the world? The position of the mainstream Trinitarian churches is that 'yes' has always been, and still is, the answer that God has given us to those questions. If we were faced for the first time with the need to frame a statement of faith, we might not have used the same words as those who produced the creeds – and the same could be said of people of many times and cultures; but through the creeds, thanks to the work of the thinkers of seventeen centuries ago, we can declare something of the true nature of God. The three-ness of God, the Trinity, is not an abstract remote concept, but a reality that touches the lives of Christians and breathes through the life of the Church. God draws us into a love that has its origin in him. And the creeds invite us to celebrate God's dealings with humanity, making and remaking us for his love's sake.

An additional note on the words 'And the Son'

Christians agree that the Spirit proceeds from the Father, as was stated in the original versions of the Nicene Creed. The question arose whether the Spirit proceeds from the Son as well. Some answered 'no', because the relationship described as 'proceeding' is distinctive to the Spirit and the Father: that most closely reflects Jesus' words in John 14. Others answered 'yes', because of texts such as John 20.22, which we mentioned earlier. At the risk of over-simplifying what happened, we can say that the church of western Europe (led by Rome) said 'yes' to the question whether the Spirit proceeds from the Son as well as the Father; the Greek and other churches of the east said 'no'. And so, at the end of the phrase in the Creed which originally stated that the Spirit 'proceeds from the Father', the western or 'Latin' church added 'and the Son' (in Latin, *Filioque*).

Debate about exactly what is meant by all of these words has never come to an end (especially over the various possible nuances of 'proceed'). It has been the cause of disagreement between the churches of east and west, and there was a bitter division between the two in the early Middle Ages, partly because the eastern churches do not agree that the additional words 'and the Son' express the truth, and partly because the eastern churches have been unhappy at the fact that the western church unilaterally changed the words of the Creed. In our own times, when there has been dialogue between theologians from east and west, a large element in their discussions has been to work towards a greater understanding on this issue. It is probably fair to say that many western Christian theologians are sympathetic to the eastern tradition on this point – more so than might be suggested by our 'western heritage', and by the fact that the words 'and the Son' stand in the 'normal' versions of the Creed printed in most service books. In outline, this story explains why the Nicene Creed as used in Roman Catholic, Anglican and many other western churches traditionally includes the words 'and the Son', but some more recently authorized or optional versions of the Creed revert to the 'pre-*Filioque*' form and miss those words out.

To think about further

One of the prayers used at the end of the Eucharist asks God to 'send us out in the power of your Spirit to live and work to your praise and glory'. What does living and working in the power of the Spirit mean from day to day?

Part 3: Telling God's story

8

Celebrating God's plan (i)

My soul doth magnify the Lord

In the next three chapters we're going to look at some passages from the Bible that have been borrowed word-for-word into its services. They will be especially familiar to anyone who knows the Church's forms of morning and evening worship. These passages of Scripture open the way to major themes in the Christian faith. And since we are looking at 'words and worship' together, this is an opportunity to think of what it means for the Church to have 'adopted' these texts as part of daily worship, and for them to be repeated thousands upon thousands of times by millions of people.

The texts are usually called by the first words in their Latin versions: *Magnificat, Benedictus* and *Nunc dimittis. Benedictus* (Blessed be the Lord God of Israel) features in morning prayer. We find *Magnificat* (My soul doth magnify the Lord) and *Nunc dimittis* (Lord, now lettest thou thy servant depart in peace) in *Book of Common Prayer* Evensong: or, in some other service patterns, *Magnificat* comes in evening prayer and *Nunc dimittis* in a separate service of night prayer.

These three passages all come from Luke's Gospel. Luke's two-volume account (his Gospel and the Acts of the Apostles) leads us from the time before Jesus was born, all the way to the stage where the good news of Jesus was spreading around the countries of the Mediterranean. The thread running all the way through both volumes is Luke's very strong idea of God's plan, which has been at work in his chosen people, Israel, and which is becoming a reality in the lives of people throughout the world. Luke is a wonderful narrator. When he wants to tell us about God's plan, he writes stories rather than anything that reads like an article or an essay. He begins his Gospel with a long introduction, centred on the story of Jesus' birth and childhood. He includes three set pieces where one of the characters in the story makes some kind of speech. The three people are Mary the mother of Jesus, Zechariah the father of John the Baptist, and Simeon, an old man in the temple in Jerusalem.

Luke's introduction is like those clips at the beginning of an episode of a television serial that remind us of 'the story so far'. Each of these speeches that Luke gives us is full of Old Testament words, phrases and ideas, and we can hear echoes of the style of the psalms. There certainly is something strongly poetic about them and, although they were not written to be set to music, they are sometimes called the 'songs' of Mary, Zechariah and Simeon: which explains why they are called *canticles* (from the Latin word for a short song). And in fact they are often sung, rather than spoken, in church services.

So let's look at each of these speeches or canticles in turn, and in the order they occur in Luke's Gospel. We'll think about the text itself, about its context in the Gospel, and about the fact that it is 'owned' by the Church through the way it is used in services (its *liturgical* use). We shall use here the translation found in the Prayer Book, because that is the version that many readers will be used to.

Magnificat

The first canticle to look at is Mary's song, *Magnificat*, and we shall begin by reminding ourselves of the background. Luke introduces his readers to Mary in a scene ('the Annunciation', Luke 1.26–38) where the angel Gabriel is sent to her from God. Gabriel greets Mary as 'favoured ... The Lord is with you.' Mary is at first perplexed, but learns of God's plan and the part that she has in it. Amid Mary's confusion and wonder, Gabriel has told her what is going to happen: 'you will conceive' (Luke 1.31). Gabriel does not invite or ask Mary whether she will agree, but talks to her in terms of a straightforward announcement. She is to bear a child who will be called 'the Son of the Most High' and whom she must name Jesus, 'God saves'. At the end of the scene, Mary puts herself into God's hands as she says, 'Behold the servant of the Lord: let it be with me according to your word.' The angel departs. In the way that Luke tells the story, Mary gives her consent to something which is certainly going to happen, because it is already in God's purposes: there is a coming together of God's will and Mary's human will. Mary goes to the house of her relative Elizabeth, who is already pregnant with her son John. Luke writes that Elizabeth was filled with the Holy Spirit and greets Mary as 'the mother of my Lord'. Mary then says the words we know as *Magnificat*.

My soul doth magnify the Lord : and my spirit hath rejoiced in God my Saviour.

For he hath regarded : the lowliness of his handmaiden.

For behold, from henceforth : all generations shall call me blessed.

For he that is mighty hath magnified me : and holy is his Name.

And his mercy is on them that fear him : throughout all generations.

He hath shewed strength with his arm : he hath scattered the proud in the imagination of their hearts.

He hath put down the mighty from their seat : and hath exalted the humble and meek.

He hath filled the hungry with good things : and the rich he hath sent empty away.

He remembering his mercy hath holpen his servant Israel : as he promised to our forefathers, Abraham and his seed, for ever.

In the first half of *Magnificat*, Mary praises God because he has looked favourably on her: 'all generations shall call me blessed,' she declares. There is a change of mood into the second half, in which Mary does not refer specifically to herself any more. Beginning with 'He hath shewed strength with his arm', this part tells of God's power, and the changes that he brings about. *Magnificat* ends by telling how God has come to the aid of his servant Israel, in accordance with his promises to his people from ancient times. Abraham is named specifically, because he is the figure who particularly symbolizes this relationship of promise between God and his chosen nation.

Mary's words come at a crucial point in the Gospel story. It is the time at which she knows that her life will never be the same again: she now knows what her destiny is, as the mother of the one who is to be known as 'the son of the Most High'. But this is not a time of significance for Mary alone. The time is now set for the appearance of Jesus, who is the central character in the whole of human history.

Hannah and Mary

We mentioned earlier that Luke pours material borrowed from the Old Testament into these speeches in the opening part of his Gospel. The fact that he does so underlines the theme of God's dealings with his people spreading throughout time. God's plan stretches from ancient times into the future, and revolves around the events of Jesus' life. It fits this scheme then that Mary's words are based on a great speech by a woman in the Old Testament: the prayer of Hannah, the mother of Samuel (1 Sam. 2.1–10). There is some similarity, to the extent that both Hannah's and Mary's speeches are connected with the birth of a child, but the two women's situations are different. The background to Hannah's prayer is that for years she had been taunted by Peninnah – the other wife of her husband Elkanah – because she was childless. Hannah comes to the shrine of God at Shiloh, where she is found by Eli who at first mistakes Hannah's prayers for drunken ramblings. But when Eli hears Hannah's story he promises her that she will have a son of her own. In time, Hannah does indeed have a son – Samuel, a name which comes from the word meaning 'ask', because as she says, 'I asked him of the Lord.' Hannah brings Samuel to Eli to be 'given to the Lord'. Hannah then makes her speech.

Hannah's speech (actually the Hebrew text calls it a prayer) is a victory song, strong and uncompromising. It takes delight in God's strength and his conquest of his enemies. 'My heart exults in the Lord! My power rises up in the Lord!' (1 Sam. 2.1). The prayer goes on to celebrate how the mighty are defeated and the feeble gain strength. Those who were full are ruined but the hungry are fat. The barren has borne seven, but the one with many children is bereft. God guards the faithful but cuts off the wicked. After the first few words, Hannah's prayer moves on from her own situation to a wide-ranging celebration of God's favour towards those who suffer injustice: the theme is the all-encompassing power of God, how he restores the fortunes of those who are crushed and powerless, and puts down those who have had everything.

The tone of Hannah's prayer explains a lot about *Magnificat*, and certainly the mood-change in the middle, where Mary's words become much more like Hannah's strong claims in tone. And there is another connection between Hannah's prayer and Mary's *Magnificat*. Unfortunately it tends to get lost in translation. At an earlier stage of the story (1 Sam. 1.11), Hannah has prayed that God will look on the woeful situation that she is in. The ancient Greek version of the Old Testament, the Septuagint, uses the word *tapeinōsis*, which comes from the basic meaning 'low' and can mean being in a low state, dejection, lowliness or humility. In the second verse of *Magnificat*, we find that Mary praises God because he has regarded her *tapeinōsis* – which the Prayer Book translates as lowliness. There is no single word in English that gets the sense both of Hannah's distress and Mary's humility, which explains why translators of English Bibles use different words in each place, although the Greek word is the same. Luke links his text to Hannah's prayer more closely than translations tend to reveal.

The model for *Magnificat*, then, is the triumphant cry to God from the feisty mother of one of Israel's great heroes. Perhaps we should bear that in mind as we approach not only *Magnificat* but also the person of Mary. There is a danger of over-sentimentalizing Mary. Of all the qualities that she has been thought of as symbolizing, the one we must not lose sight of is her co-operation with the will of God: an active, rational, positive and even *strong* kind of obedience. More than that, she stands as a symbol of what it means to have a particular calling to serve God, in a way that is necessary to the outworking of his plan: fulfilling a crucial role at a critical time.

The principle in all this is that God acts with justice, and intervenes in his world. Centuries ago God rescued Hannah from her distress and sent his representative Samuel for the sake of the people of Israel: the same God is now acting again by sending Jesus for the sake of the world. The old themes of Hannah's prayer are renewed and refreshed in *Magnificat*, where we are told that the proud are scattered, the mighty deposed, the humble and meek raised up, the hungry filled and the rich sent empty away.

Making Mary's words our own

What are we doing as the Church, by taking Mary's words and then saying them every evening? What does it mean when in our cathedral services we clothe them day by day in the music of various times and styles and cultures? What about the way we take the intensely personal 'my' and 'me' of the first part of Mary's song and make it the song of the whole Church? By singing the song of Mary, the Church is not merely saying 'thank you God for the woman in whose womb Jesus grew and on whose mouth these words were placed' – though yes, there is always something of that element, as the Church honours Mary in her role as God's servant. Following Mary's example, we are each God's servants and we have to take the responsibility of recognizing that he has work which is specifically and specially ours to carry out: being ready to fulfil our role at the time God calls us. And constantly, daily, the Church together makes its own pledge, as it says of itself, 'Behold the servant of the Lord.' The Church as a corporate body has a calling to tell the good news of Jesus, to live and worship in accordance with God's will, and to be part of God's mission by making a difference in his world in his name.

It's helpful to keep Hannah's prayer as the model for *Magnificat* in mind, because it means we are more likely to appreciate the sense of power that is an essential element of *Magnificat* – and not only of the text of *Magnificat* itself but also the story in which Luke frames it, and the truth that it is pointing us towards. Following Hannah's model, the last part of *Magnificat* challenges us to think what the principles are by which God intends us to live. In saying *Magnificat* again and again, whether individually or as a Church, we make its message one that we own, which means we must take on the responsibilities it brings. It has been said that *Magnificat* is not so much a case of God turning the ways of the world upside down, as turning them the right way up. Ways that are contrary to his will are shown to be false. Lives are to be lived and relationships are to be conducted in accordance with God's will: but that involves a challenge to so many of those flawed assumptions, habits and patterns into which humanity lapses. We mustn't forget that *Magnificat* comes at a key moment in Luke's whole account of how God sent his Messiah into the world: in that sense it is primarily about Jesus rather than Mary. Luke is preparing us for the age of the Messiah, the time when people will see what God's way of being and living truly is.

That is why we need to see *Magnificat* as a text that both comforts and disturbs. It is possible to distort its message by interpreting it in either of two extreme ways: one, reducing it to a manifesto for social action, the other consigning it to a 'spiritual' realm in which anything difficult or challenging is treated as a figure of speech rather than touching on everyday reality. It is a travesty to repeat the words that God has filled the hungry and not address the fact that that there are hungry people: and, whoever we are, it is defeatist to think that we are not in a position to be able to bring at least some influence to bear on the global scandal of injustices. (A friend visited a farm in Africa and asked the farmer, 'Does Fair Trade make any difference to you?' 'Yes,' he said, 'it means my children can go to school now.') It is futile to sing about how God has put down the proud and the mighty, and exalted the humble and meek, if we are oblivious of the power-play in which we are involved. Worse, it is a denial of what *Magnificat* is telling us about God if we acquiesce in such things in the life of the Church. It is so easy to fall unwittingly into habits of self-justification that push the harder challenges of *Magnificat* away so that they do not fully impinge on ourselves and our own interests.

Music

Magnificat and other canticles are often set to music, and there is a repertoire of settings in many languages in many styles and dating from many different centuries. We can see a parallel between what we do when we sing liturgical texts and what happens when an artist creates a painting. It adds a dimension of art and beauty. It also calls attention to the subject, and in that way gives it a special prominence or substance. And it also means that the words or subject, which may come from a past age, are lifted into the age of the composer or artist. The centuries are spanned. And when music is recreated by being taken from the page and turned into sound, there is a stronger bond of creativity again between past and present. Making a setting of *Magnificat* and performing it can symbolize the ongoing creative potential, relevance and challenge that are found in the words.

Magnificat and its place in worship

Magnificat moves us to thank God for Mary, and to be in awe of the way God involves people in his plan for the world. It is an important part of the continuity between the Old and New Testaments. It draws us into the tradition of the Old Testament prophets and their call for peace, mercy and justice, and it points to Jesus in his identity as Messiah. There is an added dimension that comes from the fact that, in the *Book of Common Prayer* order for evening prayer, *Magnificat* links the readings from the Old and New Testaments. As Mary celebrates and looks forward to the birth of her son, so *Magnificat* invites us to honour the Old Testament heritage, and then to welcome the coming of Christ, whose presence in the world is witnessed to in the reading from the New Testament. And if we have the will to celebrate his coming and the eagerness to hear his good news, we need also the courage to hear the challenge of the gospel and understand that to live according to the way of Christ is to be ready to change.

To think about further

Read through Hannah's prayer (1 Sam. 2.1–10) and then *Magnificat*. Does it change the way you think of *Magnificat* (or the way that you picture Mary)?

9

Celebrating God's plan (ii)

Blessed be the Lord God of Israel

For parents, the birth of a child is a time like no other. *Blessed be the Lord God of Israel* are the opening words of a passage that is spoken by a father at the naming of a very special, week-old baby boy. Luke shows us not only the joy that any proud father would have but also the joy of someone who knows that an important event in moving God's plan for humankind forward has taken place. This is a passage that ties themes from the Old Testament into the New: it honours the relationship that God has had with Israel through history, as the foundation for the coming of the Messiah. It is this text, *Benedictus*, the second of Luke's poetic passages, that the Church uses in worship (Luke 1.68–79).

The background to the passage in the Bible is this. We meet Zechariah, a priest, and his wife Elizabeth, who is related to Mary. An angel has brought a message to Zechariah promising that, despite both he and his wife Elizabeth being old, they will have a son who will 'make ready a people prepared for the Lord' (Luke 1.17) and whom they must name John (meaning 'the Lord is gracious'). Zechariah apparently fails to believe the message, so the angel says that he will be unable to speak until the events foretold occur. In the course of time, Elizabeth gives birth to her son. The time comes to name him, and in accordance with the angel's instructions Elizabeth insists that he be called John. Her relatives and neighbours object – it is the custom to name a child after a family member, and no relative is called John – but Zechariah settles the matter by writing down: 'His name is John.' Immediately Zechariah is able to speak and praises God. The people's reaction to all this is to recognize that the hand of the Lord was with John. Luke tells the whole story to make it clear that God is involved in every aspect of this sequence of events. The Holy Spirit is at work – in fact, the angel told Zechariah that his son would be filled with the Holy Spirit from before the time of his birth. And, filled with the Holy Spirit (Luke writes), Zechariah prophesied, saying:

> Blessed be the Lord God of Israel : for he hath visited, and redeemed his people;
>
> And hath raised up a mighty salvation for us : in the house of his servant David;
>
> As he spake by the mouth of his holy Prophets : which have been since the world began;
>
> That we should be saved from our enemies : and from the hands of all that hate us;
>
> To perform the mercy promised to our forefathers : and to remember his holy covenant;
>
> To perform the oath which he sware to our forefather Abraham : that he would give us;
>
> That we being delivered out of the hands of our enemies : might serve him without fear;
>
> In holiness and righteousness before him : all the days of our life.
>
> And thou, child, shalt be called the Prophet of the Highest : for thou shalt go before the face of the Lord to prepare his ways;
>
> To give knowledge of salvation unto his people : for the remission of their sins;
>
> Through the tender mercy of our God : whereby the day-spring from on high hath visited us;
>
> To give light to them that sit in darkness, and in the shadow of death : and to guide our feet into the way of peace.

Telling the truth through a story

What kind of story is this? Is it a factual report of a real occurrence? Or is it all Luke's invention? That is to ask the question in a way that belongs to our own time and culture rather than Luke's, and it is to set up a false distinction between things that we might think of as 'literally true', as if all others are 'untrue'. Luke has a purpose in writing as he does, which is to tell his readers the truth about John; and, since John is the forerunner of Jesus, Luke is actually telling us at one remove things about Jesus himself. At the stage where this passage comes in the Gospel, the Messiah has not yet appeared, but it is now sure that he will, because John, who is destined to be his forerunner and herald, has been born. The world is poised for a new future, and it will come with all the certainty of something that has been planned and put into action by God himself. Zechariah's outpouring of prophecy is not only – or not so much – the declaration of a man at the birth of his son: it is also the testimony that belongs to one specific time, when God's promises are on the point of being fulfilled.

Old and new

Benedictus has the air of a speech that someone has been bursting to make. In the story, Zechariah has been prevented from talking for a while, and, when he regains his speech, the words of *Benedictus* flow from his mouth. But perhaps Luke intends us to see a deeper symbolism. Luke says that Zechariah and Elizabeth were righteous and lived blamelessly according to the requirements of the Jewish Law (Luke 1.8): so we can see them as standing for all that is good and honourable about the Jewish people. They represent the faithful tradition of keeping God's commandments and living day to day in the way laid down in the Law, maintained in the face of all the opposition and persecution that Jews had suffered through the years. Faithful Jews looked to the time when it would be possible to greet the forerunner of the Messiah, the one who would have the 'spirit and power of Elijah' to signal the coming of God's Anointed and to turn the hearts of the people to obedience (Luke 1.17, which echoes Malachi 4.5–6). Now, with the birth of John, the time is here to unlock that pent-up impulse to praise God for the coming of the new age, which had been held waiting for generations. And since Zechariah blesses God as the 'God of Israel', Luke is encouraging his readers to acknowledge and celebrate God's dealings with his people from ancient times. Whatever is to come, and wherever the message of the gospel is to spread throughout the world, it is rooted in what God has done so far. Christianity is grafted into the rootstock of the Jewish heritage.

Themes in *Benedictus*

In the *Book of Common Prayer* version of *Benedictus*, Zechariah praises God for 'visiting' and redeeming his people. 'Visit' means much more here than 'come to see someone and then go away again'. Its older sense (and this gets the sense of Luke's Greek word)[11] means to get involved at first hand with full authority. The words translated 'set them free'[12] literally mean 'made redemption (or ransom) for his people'. The theme is God's close involvement in the world, and the mission that he undertakes to establish a lasting relationship between humanity and himself. So these words make it clear that God is not in any sense remote or indifferent: he doesn't confine his interest or activity to some realm called 'heaven' and keep himself aloof from humanity and human needs. God has 'raised up a mighty salvation for us', proclaims Zechariah. In Chapter 6 we looked in outline at the idea of salvation. It is interesting that the words of *Benedictus* are that God has raised up salvation, rather than a saviour: Zechariah's words point to the effect of what God will do. The reference to the ancestry of King David picks up the idea that the Messiah will be of royal descent, and Luke makes it clear elsewhere that Mary's husband Joseph was

---

11 *epeskepsato*: among other translations, 'look favourably' (NRSV) is not quite right and the Greek word has a more specific meaning than is suggested by *Common Worship*'s 'come'.

12 *epoiēsen lutrōsin*.

a descendant of David (Luke 2.4; 3.31). God's rescue of humanity, which is a long way from anything that could be achieved through military success, replaces earthly ideas of kingly rule and political deliverance.

Prophecy begins again

Zechariah's prophecy tells how all this is in accord with God's words through his holy prophets from ages ago. So again, Luke is inviting us to see complete continuity between what God has done in time past and what he is doing in the present. By describing the prophets as 'holy', Luke is once more emphasizing how God's plan has been in place from before the ages began: God has been guiding the people who spoke in his name and declared his will, brought his message to the people and encouraged them to understand his ways and what he required of them. Luke has already told us specifically that Zechariah is 'prophesying' now: Luke intends his readers to understand that *Benedictus* is the latest in the series of pronouncements of prophets going back through the centuries. The great age of the Old Testament prophets was hundreds of years earlier, and since then there had been a yearning for a revival of the prophetic spirit. With Zechariah's speech, the age of prophecy begins again, just as the destiny of Israel and the purposes of God are coming to a uniquely significant point.

Peace and promise

The next few words appear to open up a new idea: they speak of God saving his people 'from our enemies and from the hands of all that hate us'.[13] Why is the theme of rescue from enemies so prominent in *Benedictus*? The statement that there would be such a rescue seems at face value to run counter to what actually happened. In the most obvious terms, the people of Israel were

---

13 The word-order of Luke's Greek doesn't transfer well to English, which explains why the translations we use differ so much.

not rescued from their enemies in the following years. And the early Church had plenty of opponents and sometimes actual enemies. Perhaps the answer lies in the section between the two places in *Benedictus* which mention enemies. Zechariah speaks of the mercy promised to 'our forefathers', God remembering the 'holy covenant', and the oath which God swore to 'our forefather Abraham'. Here are themes of identity, faith and promise, of the mutual relationship between God and the people. The words of *Benedictus* are calculated to spark off memories from the Old Testament. For instance, in Genesis 26.4–5, God appears to Isaac and renews the oath he made to Abraham, that his descendants will be as many as the stars, and 'all the nations of the earth shall gain blessing for themselves through your offspring, because Abraham obeyed my voice'. God's word to Jeremiah (Jer. 11.5) is that he intends to 'perform the oath that I swore to your ancestors, to give them a land flowing with milk and honey'. The final verse of the book of Micah describes God's compassion and forgiveness and his loyalty to Abraham (Mic. 7.20). In Deuteronomy 12.10 the promise that the people of Israel will cross the Jordan to take possession of the promised land is coupled with the assurance of having rest from enemies all around and living in safety.

How do these themes connect together? It is because from ancient times, security and stability were thought of as prerequisites for living in holiness and righteousness (Deut. 4.14) and for worshipping God as he desires. So Zechariah's words about being out of danger from enemies are part of a long-established notion of what is needed in order to live as God's people. But – here we are moving into a new age – when the Messiah comes, everything about what it means to be God's people will be refashioned. God's promises will take another form from giving the nation of Israel their own land, because his promises will be available to all the people of the earth, who will be blessed through the Messiah as Abraham's offspring. And what are the 'enemies' that we expect the Messiah to overcome? Another thread in the New Testament gives a suggestion. Paul, himself picking up a phrase from the psalms, proclaims that the Christ, the Messiah, 'must reign until he has put all his enemies under his feet. The last enemy to be destroyed is death' (1 Cor. 15.25–26; Ps. 110.1). The gift of life that the Messiah brings is the final and complete rescue from everything that is destructive, and everything that gets in the way of a relationship with God, including that ultimate force of separation and destruction – death itself.

Looking forward to John's ministry

Zechariah greets his son John, who in his adult ministry will be 'called the prophet of the Highest, for thou shalt go before the face of the Lord to prepare his ways'. John is to be the 'voice' crying out (Isa. 40.3), bringing a message to a people and to Jerusalem in need of comfort – reassurance and the knowledge that God promises to bring restoration (Isa. 40.1). In his own ministry, John will prepare the way of the Lord in that he will prepare the way for Jesus (Mark 1.2–8). The implication of the words in *Benedictus* is that the coming of Christ is the coming of God – so these words are looking beyond John to Jesus.

Benedictus and the Messiah

Expectation and fulfilment is the key to the next line of *Benedictus*: 'the dayspring [or dawn] from on high' (that is, from God). The theme comes from the last chapter of Malachi – a book that is full of anticipation and a sense of looking forward to the time when God will act. 'For you who revere my name the sun of righteousness shall rise, with healing in its wings' (Mal. 4.2 – you will probably have recognized this verse as the source of the line 'Hail the Sun of Righteousness' in the Christmas hymn 'Hark! the herald angels sing'). This dawning sun will 'visit' us, and, yes, the word is the same in the Greek as the one we met at the beginning of *Benedictus*, describing the God of Israel's close involvement with humankind. Putting the ideas together, the Messiah as the envoy of God's righteousness will come among his people with authority and power. This will all happen 'in the tender compassion of our God' – God's mercy and yearning for his people. The one who is this 'rising' – the Messiah – will give light (that is, will bring the knowledge of God) to those who are in darkness and the shadow of death. He will 'guide our feet into the way of peace'. He will be the antidote to the crisis that is described in the last part of the book of Isaiah (59.8–10) in terms of people not knowing the way of peace, lacking justice and righteousness, and being in the dark. Here in *Benedictus* is the answer: the assurance that God has not forgotten his people and that the time has come for him to act decisively in the person of the Messiah.

Benedictus is a wonderful poetic text. Like a lot of poems, it doesn't give us a direct description of its real subject: because although Luke's setting is Zechariah greeting his son John, and the words Jesus, Christ and Messiah don't occur in *Benedictus*, it is really all about what God is about to do through the coming of Christ into the world. It is the references to the Old Testament that unlock the meaning of *Benedictus*, and so it very powerfully bridges the worlds of the Old Testament and the New (as, actually, do the figures of Zechariah and John the Baptist).

In the church's services, we say or sing *Benedictus* at the end of the sequence of psalms and Bible readings used in Morning Prayer. When we do that, it is as if we stand with Zechariah as he gives this great outpouring of praise in *Benedictus* – a great 'Yes!' to everything that God has done in the past, to what he is doing in the present, and (on the brink of a new age) to the fulfilment of his purposes in the future.

To think about further

How can Christians value and honour the Old Testament, giving it an integrity and standing of its own, and not only as a prelude to the New Testament?

10

Celebrating God's plan (iii)

Lord, now lettest thou thy servant depart in peace

Strength and comfort

The setting of the third of Luke's canticles, *Nunc dimittis* (Luke 2.29–32), is the Jerusalem Temple, and unlike the other two canticles takes us to a time after Jesus was born. Here we are shown two elderly people with special insight, first Simeon and then Anna. There's a particular poignancy about the scene. Simeon knows that his life is drawing to an end. Luke tells us how Simeon was devout and had been looking for the consolation or comforting of Israel. So he was a man who not only observed the Jewish Law carefully but also cherished the hope that God would act decisively on behalf of his people and that there would be a revival of Israel's role as God's chosen nation. Luke uses the same word for consolation or comfort as the one that the Greek version of the Old Testament uses at the beginning of Isaiah 40: 'Comfort, comfort my people'; and at Isaiah 49.13: 'Sing for joy … For the Lord has comforted his people'. This meaning of 'comfort' includes not only reassurance and healing but also encouragement and strengthening for action (just as the *fort* in *comfort* means 'strong'). When Luke tells us that Simeon was looking for the consolation of Israel, it is in the sense of Israel fulfilling its destiny and being its true self again – it doesn't mean anything on the lines of being settled down into passive inactivity.

Luke weaves a triple mention of the Holy Spirit into the scene about Simeon. He does this to make it as clear as possible that Simeon's actions and words are a special gift from God: and that just as the Spirit has been active in Simeon's previous life as a righteous and devout man, now it is the Spirit who draws him to this moment and this place. First, he says that the Holy Spirit rested on Simeon. Second, the Holy Spirit had revealed to Simeon that he would not die until he had seen the Lord's Messiah. And third, Simeon comes into the Temple at Jerusalem 'in the Spirit' (Luke 2.27) at the time when Mary and Joseph come there with the baby Jesus for Mary to perform the ceremony that marked the end of the time of 40 days following the birth of a son, as required in the Law (Lev. 12). So the Temple, which carries all the symbolism of the meeting place between God and humankind, is the setting for the meeting between Jesus the Lord's Messiah and Simeon, who represents the yearning of humanity in general, and Israel in particular, for God. Simeon now recognizes Jesus as the Messiah, takes him in his arms, and speaks these words:

> Lord, now lettest thou thy servant depart in peace : according to thy word.
> For mine eyes have seen : thy salvation;
> Which thou hast prepared : before the face of all people;
> To be a light to lighten the Gentiles : and to be the glory of thy people Israel.

There is no hint of regret or distress in *Nunc dimittis*. Rather, there is a sense of fulfilment and of God's promise coming true. Simeon acknowledges that God is letting him approach death in peace – peace in the full sense of wholeness and completion – in accordance with the promise that God has given him.

Before all people

Simeon says that he has seen the salvation which God has prepared 'before the face of all people'. Those words may seem strange. In what sense has God done anything here in full view of all people? It is not as if the world has noticed the birth of this child. The clue again is in the Old Testament, because words from the book of Isaiah have been borrowed and rearranged: 'the Lord has comforted his people, he has redeemed Jerusalem. The Lord has bared his holy arm *before the eyes of all the nations*; and all the ends of the earth *shall see the salvation* of our God' (Isa. 52.9–10). The message of Isaiah is that God's action – salvation – will be seen by all nations. Simeon recognizes that the birth of Jesus signals the beginning of this coming into effect. True, the nations have not yet experienced the result of the Messiah coming into the world, but they will in due time: what has happened so far, the birth of the Messiah, is part of God's plan. There is no room for doubt: for God has set the sequence of his action going, and that is the guarantee that the whole of it will come to fruition. And this is underlined in the way that Luke shows us Simeon saying that he has seen God's *salvation*, rather than greeting Jesus personally as the *saviour* – using the turn of phrase taken from Isaiah (and incidentally mirroring the expression Zechariah uses in *Benedictus* that we looked at in the previous chapter).

Light for the nations: glory for Israel

In the last part of Simeon's speech, we meet some key-words that point us again to the Old Testament, and specifically to the second half of the book of Isaiah. The point of these closing lines is that the Messiah is God's gift both to his ancient people of Israel and also to the whole of humankind.[14] So Simeon's words emphasize that what God is doing for all the nations, and what he is doing (and has done) for Israel, cannot be separated one from the other, but both need to be seen as a single gift to humanity: and that gift takes the form of flesh and blood, the child Jesus in his arms. 'Light of the nations' is a phrase that comes twice in the book of Isaiah, in 42.6 and in 49.6, from which *Nunc dimittis*

---

14 'Gentiles' is a translation of the Greek word *ethn* which means 'nations' – think of 'ethnic' in English – and is used in the Bible as a technical term for non-Jews.

picks up an old theme: being the servant of God for the sake of Israel alone is 'too light a thing ... I will give you as a light to the nations, that my salvation may reach to the end of the earth'.

And as far as Israel is concerned, in Isaiah 46.13, God promises that he 'will put salvation in Zion, for Israel my glory'. So Simeon tells us, in effect, that the appearance of God's salvation (the Messiah) in Zion (Jerusalem) is a sign of God's glory. We should remember that Luke is writing a two-volume story from before the birth of Jesus to the time when the Church was taking root in many nations. Simeon's words compress the essence of the matter into a few words: the destiny of Israel and the promise held out to all the nations of the world are one and the same, and they will come to fruition through the Messiah's coming and his work. Luke shows Simeon as a prophetic, Spirit-filled figure who has an insight into this 'light' and 'glory': he has recognized the whole of that in the otherwise relatively unremarkable event of a couple walking into the Temple with a young baby.

The scene goes on further from the words of *Nunc dimittis* itself. Luke tells us that Mary and Joseph were amazed at what was being said about Jesus. That in itself is interesting – because already in his Gospel Luke has said how they had been told many times that this was no normal child. But they are still surprised by Simeon's words. Joseph and Mary have a lot of learning to do yet, about who this child is and how he is going to fulfil his destiny (Luke 2.41–52). Simeon blesses them and then speaks specifically to Mary in words that give a foretaste of what Jesus' work and ministry will cost. 'This child', he says, 'is destined for the falling and the rising of many in Israel, and to be a sign that will be opposed so that the inner thoughts of many will be revealed.' This is not a direct quotation from the Old Testament, but it echoes Isaiah 8.13–15 where there is a warning that the Lord will be 'a rock one stumbles over', a trap and a snare. Yes, God loves his people, but that never means that God sets aside his awesome nature: an encounter with God brings with it the prospect of judgement and potentially even danger, as well as the promise of his saving and rescuing power. So it is with the coming of the Messiah. Simeon celebrates the arrival of God's Messiah on the world's scene, but also hints that the time of challenge and truth, judgement and crisis is coming. Inner thoughts will be revealed because the time for falsehood and deception is gone: under God's judgement, even thoughts and motives will be shown for what they are.

Simeon and Mary

In one of the most moving sentences of the New Testament, Simeon says to Mary: 'And a sword will pierce your own heart too.' In thirty or so years' time, Mary is to undergo that most painful experience of seeing her own son suffer and die. In Luke's Greek and in some older translations this phrase about the 'sword' breaks into the middle of what Simeon has to say about Jesus: '... a sign that will be opposed – and a sword will pierce your own heart too – so that the inner thoughts of many will be revealed'. Many recent translations change the phrase order so that the 'sword in the heart' sentence is separated from the rest of what Simeon says. Maybe that makes for smoother English: but it takes away the sense of Simeon suddenly finding his own thoughts about Jesus interrupted by words that he says to Mary about her own future. In Luke's Greek, it is as if the words hurt Simeon when he says them as much as Mary when she hears them, but they force their way through and interrupt the rest of what he is telling her.

Looking forward

In the temple, with the family and Simeon, is the prophet Anna. Luke does not report any of her words directly, but tells of her life-long devotion and how she stays constantly in the temple praying. Anna begins to tell 'all who were looking for the redemption of Jerusalem' about Jesus. 'The redemption of Jerusalem' is an idea we have met already, as part of a text (Isa. 52.9) which supplied words and themes for *Nunc dimittis*. Luke's words about 'all who were looking' fits in with other evidence we have about the time when Jesus was born, when many people were hoping for God to act in a decisive way, to turn round the fortunes of the Jewish people which had sunk so low.

Talking about the Messiah

Once more Luke is showing us the importance of the Old Testament heritage and background. Simeon and Anna are witnessing to the centuries-old aspiration of God showing his power again for the sake of the people Israel. But already as we have seen in the later chapters of the book of Isaiah, and elsewhere too, the theme starts to develop of the Jewish people having a special place and role among the nations, because of their having a special relationship with God: 'In those days ten men from nations of every language shall take hold of a Jew, grasping his garment and saying, "Let us go with you, for we have heard that God is with you"' (Zech. 8.23). As Simeon and Anna see the child Jesus and recognize him for who he is, they stand on the threshold of the time when the Jewish heritage becomes the setting for God's new definitive activity in the world.

And let us not lose sight of the significance of Simeon and Anna being old, because it is important in itself. Simeon has hinted at his expectation that he will die – maybe soon – now that he has seen the Messiah. Simeon and Anna will have died before Jesus grows to adulthood, and they will not see the events that God intends will happen in the decades to come. But they have the vision to catch the importance of the moment when the infant Jesus enters the temple, and their words contain celebration and fulfilment. They know, without a trace of regret or bitterness, that others will see how God's plans come to fruition, but they themselves will not.

Saying *Nunc dimittis*

The Church uses *Nunc dimittis* daily, as the canticle at late evening worship (Compline) or as the second canticle at *Book of Common Prayer* Evensong. Each of those positions has a rationale. To take its use in Compline first, Simeon's words address the subject of death – for him, a death that has a sense of completion, contentment and joy. He places himself in God's hands as he expects his life to come to a close. Since sleep is a symbol of death, the notion of commending ourselves to God in sleep as in death gives *Nunc dimittis* a natural place in night prayer that is said before going to sleep. And if we think of the Prayer Book pattern where *Nunc dimittis* is said at Evensong, the key words of peace, salvation and glory point to this canticle being a fitting conclusion to the day's round of worship. It marks the end of the double (morning and evening) sequence of readings from the Old and New Testaments. Through that sequence, and through the medium of prayer and scripture, God has shown us his salvation: we have walked in the footsteps of Simeon and Anna, we have caught something of the sense of expectation and hope, and the fulfilment that God brought about; we have been part of recognizing the fulfilment of God's purposes, rooted in the tradition of Judaism and now moving in a new direction through the person of Jesus.

Nunc dimittis and the Church's year

Nunc dimittis has its special place in the Church's calendar as well as in daily prayer. Just as Luke tells us that these events took place 40 days after Jesus was born, so the Church celebrates the fortieth day after Christmas (2 February) as the feast of the Presentation of Christ in the Temple, sometimes called Candlemas. It draws together the theme of Jesus Christ who is both light and glory, with the recognition that judgement and suffering are also part of the story of his ministry. The day carries with it the sense of new possibility and the intentions of God being ready to be fulfilled:

'now we rejoice and glorify your name that we, too have seen your salvation'.[15]

Canticles and story

When Luke set out to tell his readers the truth about Jesus, he used the medium of story, full of references to the Old Testament. He did not write bluntly, 'Jesus is God' or 'Jesus is divine': but he took ideas and words and phrases of the Jewish Scriptures, quoting them, sometimes adapting them, reassembling them, in order to make it clear that God is present in the person of Jesus. The Gospel writers use story – and very significantly, the way in which they tell their stories – in order to tell their readers about who Jesus is, and why he and what he did and said is not only important but also *world changing*. It's as if they say, 'In order to tell you what you need to know about Jesus, I'm going to paint a scene in words' – and they give us clues in their account that enable us to see Jesus as the focal point of God's plans from ancient times, and the central figure in what is to happen in the future.

Saying the canticles

We are used to telling some stories over and over again. Think for a moment of what happens at Christmas: we have heard the story of the birth of Jesus countless times, and yet we expect to hear it again if we go to a carol service. Even if everyone present knew the story by heart, if we did *not* hear the story read to us, we would very understandably think that something was missing. There are many contexts where repeating a familiar story is important: not because it tells us anything new, but because it somehow helps to give the occasion its identity, to make it what it is.

Luke's canticles do something very similar. Every time

---

15 You may like to use some of the words for the feast of the Presentation as a meditation on *Nunc dimittis*: see *Common Worship*, pp. 306–7.

worshippers pray, we are part of a movement of prayer which is, we could say, an aspect of the *corporate* task of God's Church. So, every day, the Church corporately recites the canticles. Every day the Church re-enters the story of Zechariah, Mary, Simeon and Anna. When we repeat passages such as this, we may, helpfully, no longer find ourselves having to search in our minds for the 'right' words for prayer: but the set (or 'liturgical') texts act as a kind of 'carrier wave'. We somehow adopt their words as our own, and we can hook the more personal aspects of our thanksgiving and prayer on to them. We say our 'yes' to God as the Gospel characters said theirs; we celebrate Luke's portrait of people who recognized God at work in their own time and before their eyes and, like them, we thank God for the gift of the Messiah.

To think about further

Do you value saying the same texts over and over again in worship? Why?

Can you think of an instance where someone has been generous enough to see God at work in a project or venture, giving it their support while being aware that they themselves will not live to see it come to fruition?

Part 4: Signs of power

11

With Christ in baptism

Christ claims you for his own

Worship can be centred on actions as well as words. Some kinds of worship that we are looking at in this book are based very much on words: but in these next chapters we shall be thinking about two forms of worship in which action is essential, namely, baptism and Holy Communion. In them, the action that takes place is both a sign of God's activity and also the means by which we open ourselves to receive a gift that he gives. In the Prayer Book, the word *sacrament* is used for this blending of gift and sign, defined as 'an outward and visible sign of an inward and spiritual grace given to us, ordained by Christ himself ... and a pledge to assure us'.[16] In this chapter, then, we shall think about baptism.

Baptism through times of change

The climax of a service of baptism – the moment when baptism itself takes place – comes when the minister plunges the person to be baptized (the *candidate*) into water, or pours water over the candidate, with the words based on Jesus' command recorded at the end of Matthew's Gospel. There, Jesus tells his eleven disciples to 'go ... and make disciples of all nations, baptizing them in the name of the Father and of the Son and of the Holy Spirit' (Matt. 28.19). Obviously, then, Christian baptism goes back to the time of the Apostles. In fact, baptism as a religious action symbolizing forgiveness and a fresh start is older than the Church – that is, the

---

16 From the Catechism.

ministry that John the Baptist was carrying out (Mark 1.4–8) – but, in time, baptism 'in the name of Jesus' or 'in the name of the Father and of the Son and of the Holy Spirit' became recognizable as the distinctive and once-for-all mark of *initiation*, that is, becoming a member of the Church, the Body of Christ. In his speech at Pentecost (the day when the Holy Spirit came in power) Peter called the people to be baptized 'in the name of Jesus', and promised that they would receive forgiveness and the gift of the Holy Spirit (Acts 2.38). From the earliest days, then, Christian belief and practice is that Christ makes his Church through baptism.[17]

Through two thousand years of the Church's existence, some features of baptism have remained constant: the use of water and the words: 'I baptize you in the name of the Father and of the Son and of the Holy Spirit.' In other respects, there have been many changes and developments, which have much to do with the relationship between Christianity and society at large. From New Testament times onwards, the first generation of Christians in any place will have been converts to a faith that was new (or new to them), with people of all ages being baptized together. But when Christianity became firmly rooted in a nation or culture, and it was the norm for children to be baptized as infants, the proportion of the population that had been baptized would have been very high: in some places, say in many British villages in the Middle Ages, it is likely that the figure reached 100 per cent. And in contrast to the situation in the earliest years of the Church, the situation came about that most people would receive baptism without first making their own, first-hand, declaration of faith. Instead, their godparents spoke on their behalf as their proxies, and candidates made their own declaration when they were confirmed.

---

17 Kenneth Stevenson, 1998, *The Mystery of Baptism*, Norwich: Canterbury Press, p. 181, makes the point that in this respect baptism is prior even to the Eucharist.

While some Christians (Baptists) follow a pattern in which people are baptized only when they are old enough to make a declaration of faith for themselves, the practice of most Christian denominations today is to admit people of all ages as baptism candidates. In these Churches, it is still the case that babies form a large proportion of baptism candidates. But for all sorts of reasons, the pattern of the great majority of people being baptized as infants has changed. It is more common now than in previous decades that people will not have been baptized so young. For many people, as they grow up, their journey of faith will bring them to the point where they wish to make a personal commitment through being baptized, when they are older children, young people or adults. Sometimes whole families are baptized together. For many older candidates, baptism comes after years of serious thinking and searching: for someone who has not previously been baptized (a person can only be baptized once!) baptism can be an important milestone in a mature journey of faith.

Opportunities and questions

All this means that there is more variety about how and why people come to baptism than would have been the case, even in a recent generation. Many parents ask for their children to be baptized, even though they are not themselves regularly involved in the life of the Church. That raises questions about how to support them in responding to their request. Furthermore, because in many places the number of younger adults attending church is relatively low, some 'baptism families' are relatively unfamiliar with Church in general and what happens at a service in particular.

When we think about baptism, then, we need to take account of many different experiences and expectations. The 'traditional' pattern of a couple bringing a new-born to be baptized will still be familiar to many people, but it would be a mistake to think of it as the only definitive approach to baptism, to which all other patterns are inferior. Amid the differences, the principles that need to be kept hold are, first, that baptism is a sign of God's love and, second, that it must always be taken seriously.

If you have been present at an adult baptism (or if you are an adult candidate yourself!) you will not need telling this, but the point needs to be made very firmly: baptism is not 'kid's stuff'. That is not only because it's possible for people to be baptism candidates at any age, but because baptism, as the mark of entry into Christ's Church, is the springboard for our *life-long* disciple-ship, witness and ministry as Christians. Our worship, learning, praying and serving are firmly grounded in our baptism, from (as it may be) infancy through childhood into young adulthood and into old age. So it is important that baptism isn't marginalized, treated as something that 'doesn't matter' or 'doesn't make any difference' once you are beyond babyhood. That is the reason why the policy of the Church is that baptism should be administered 'when the most number of people come together, that the congregation … be put in mind of their own profession made to God in their baptism'.[18]

The introduction to baptism in *Common Worship* sets the scene by alluding to Jesus' words in John 3.5:

> Our Lord Jesus Christ has told us that to enter the kingdom of heaven we must be born again of water and the Spirit, and has given us baptism as the sign and seal of this new birth. Here we are washed by the Holy Spirit and made clean. Here we are clothed with Christ, dying to sin that we may live his risen life. As children of God, we have a new dignity and God calls us to fullness of life.

Signing with the cross

At the heart of this service, as we have said, is the moment of

---

18 Canon B21 of the Church of England.

baptism itself. But on the way to that moment there comes another action, when the candidate is signed with the cross. In the *Common Worship* service the minister says to the candidate:

> Christ claims you for his own.
> Receive the sign of his cross.

The minister (and others as well, if they wish) make the sign of the cross on the candidate's forehead. If others join in the signing with the cross (especially parents and godparents in the case of a very young candidate), they have a special active part in welcoming the candidate into Christ's Church. *Doing* something is likely to stick in our long-term memory in a way that what we hear, say, or read might not.

This action, and these few words, express a central truth about baptism, and they also open up the richness of symbolism that is associated with it. This mention of the cross reminds us very starkly of what it means to be a follower of Jesus Christ. The cross is the sign of Jesus' self-giving death: the sign of his love, by which he draws all people to himself (John 3.14–15; 12.32). These two phrases put a declaration of God's wonderful love side-by-side with a warning against thinking that love is cheap. So, 'Christ claims you for his own' expresses the welcoming love of God. 'Receive the sign of his cross' expresses the costliness of that same love. Baptism witnesses both to the unconditional openness of God's love and to the seriousness of the commitment that goes with love and which is an inescapable part of following Jesus. First, baptism has always been associated with repentance – Jesus calls us into a new way of living, turning away from sin and being determined to reject everything that pulls us away from God (the 'deceit and corruption of evil' as the words of the service put it). Second, there is an echo of Jesus' warning that his disciples must be prepared to deny themselves and take up their cross daily (Luke 9.23).

For candidates, parents and godparents, and for everyone else present, this is an opportunity to grasp at least something of the principles of what it means distinctively to be joined to Jesus Christ. For while there is nothing to be said against anyone living an honest and decent life (so far as that goes), there is far more to being a Christian than being a good citizen. In a country that has (thank God) been strongly influenced by Christianity for hundreds of years, and where Christian values have to a large extent influenced society at large, it is easy to fall into the pattern of thinking that there is little that marks out Christian identity amid the general opinions and habits of the population. But that can lapse into a very sloppy way of thinking about Christianity and society. It would be great if Christian values really did permeate society fully, but at all levels there is clear evidence that they do not. And conversely, it is not the task of the Church to give religious or theological respectability to whatever trend society happens to follow at any time. Being a Christian, and being the Church, does not mean setting out to be awkward or perverse, but it does mean keeping to this truth: we need God, and that need is fulfilled through Jesus, as nothing and nobody else can. In baptism we say our 'yes' to that truth, and we are invited to live it out.

Like any other act of worship, a baptism service has to be focused on God, through Jesus Christ in the power of the Spirit. But there is also a focus on the candidate, because baptism celebrates the new relationship between Jesus Christ and that person. There is something suddenly intimate about the statement that 'Christ claims *you*', and the touch with which the cross is made. 'Christ claims you for his own' speaks of a Christ who comes searching, who sees in the candidate one who has been given new birth into living hope through Christ's own resurrection (1 Peter 1.3–5). It speaks of Christ valuing and honouring and paying attention to the person who is to be baptized. It points us to the whole wonderful potential of what God can do in the future life of the candidate. And the Church has the responsibility (and the privilege) to honour and welcome the candidate in Christ's name.

And it is the candidate first and foremost who is being welcomed: in the case of a child, it skews that principle if we think the child's parents have to pass some test first. Signing with the sign of Christ is a reminder that baptism is about the *candidate's* relationship with God through Christ, and the *candidate's* membership of Christ's body.

Baptism is part of our response to the love of God, strong and unbreakable, held out to us. Baptism is first and foremost a matter of accepting a gift from God. For that reason, it is important that even when baptism candidates and their families are not regular churchgoers they find a genuine warm welcome in church. Sometimes people who do go to church regularly say of those who have been baptized: 'I wonder whether we'll see them again.' That is, however, to miss the point, because baptism is God's gift, not something the Church rations out. Welcoming newcomers in Christ's name is to take part in God's mission. And at the point of baptism we cannot know where candidates' journey of faith will lead and, if they do build up a pattern of prayer and worship, what kind of setting it will be in.[19]

United with Christ in death and life

Let us return to the text of the baptism service. In the prayer of blessing the water of baptism, the minister says:

> We thank you, Father, for the water of baptism. In it we are buried with Christ in his death. By it we share in his resurrection. Through it we are reborn by the Holy Spirit.

We've already touched on the link between baptism and the cross (and therefore with death). The theme of death and life has belonged closely to baptism from early days. Paul writes that those who are baptized 'into Christ Jesus' have been 'buried with him

---

19 See the section on Fresh Expressions in Chapter 19.

by baptism into death, so that, just as Christ was raised from the dead by the glory of the Father, so we too might walk in newness of life' (Rom. 6.3–4). Colossians 2.12 puts it even more boldly: 'when you were buried with him in baptism, you were also raised with him through faith in the power of God, who raised him from the dead'.

Baptism is about being joined to Jesus Christ — which does not mean anything by way of becoming a signed-up member of a club, but rather being joined to him in the reality and the astounding belief that he actually died, and that he truly rose. There are many other images and expressions that the New Testament uses to describe what it means to be baptized or to be joined with Christ. It tells us that when we are disciples of Christ and united with him through one baptism, we are washed and given a clean conscience (Heb. 10.22), called to grow into Christ (Eph. 4.5, 15), to be a branch of Christ the vine (John 15.5), to be a member of the Body of Christ (1 Cor. 12.27), to experience Christ's gift of the spring of water gushing up to eternal life (John 4.14). It means being part of how God has given humanity a new identity 'through Christ' and 'in Christ' (a main theme of Ephesians, for example).

Baptism and the cost of discipleship

If we ourselves have been baptized, then we have the opportunity to be reminded of our baptism and what it means, when we are present at someone else's baptism (it doesn't matter how young or old they are). It's not mere sentimentality but a powerful statement to ourselves, if we can imagine words resounding in our own head, 'Christ claims *me* for his own.' Jesus Christ loves me with a love of a kind I cannot begin to understand, and he recognizes my uniqueness in a way that even I don't have the means to do.

Being loved doesn't mean that everything the future brings will be easy. It's vanishingly unlikely that someone living in a modern Western society will experience real persecution, and find their life and liberty at risk for the sake of their faith. But anyone who takes the Christian faith seriously is likely at some point to meet opposition or even ridicule; a serious test of their integrity where issues are complicated and there is no easy solution; and there will be pressure to fit in with the view that all religion is either nonsense or bad. Young people especially have to face this, as well as the difficult questions of belief (such as why people suffer) at a stage of life when they have not built up maturity in faith. Not only some of their peers, but also many authority figures and role models will make comments or act in such a way as to discredit the Christian faith. It is essential, for the sake of people who are new or growing in the Christian faith, and for the sake of those who feel that their faith is under attack, that they receive the prayerful and practical support of the whole Church.

The drama of baptism

It has been said that what happens in a Christian's personal journey can be put in the form of four 'place words': *from, to, in* and *out*. The candidate comes *from* the world and leaves behind the way life used to be. He or she is drawn *to* God and the community of the Church. *In* the Church, the person is received, equipped and nurtured as a disciple; and, strengthened by God's Spirit, goes *out* into the world to serve God, and to serve people in his name. Baptism draws together these themes. To be baptized, to be a godparent or sponsor, simply to be present at a baptism, is to say 'yes' and 'amen' to Christ's claim on us all. As we celebrate Christ's claim in baptism, we proclaim the love of God, and we celebrate his call to serve him in the world.

To think about further

Trace a cross on your forehead and say to yourself, 'Christ claims you for his own: receive the sign of his cross.' What do those words say to you?

How is it possible to balance an 'open welcome' and 'seriousness of commitment' in relation to baptism?

How can we celebrate baptism more fully, as the mark of our shared identity and calling in Christ?

12

Sign of reconciliation

The peace of the Lord

There were many changes that took place in the Holy Communion services of many Christian churches in the 1960s and 1970s. One of them brought about a shift in the dynamic or ambience of worship that was far greater than the few words involved might have suggested: the exchange of the Peace, with the words:

The peace of the Lord be always with you;
and also with you.

Clergy and congregations were encouraged to turn and greet one another. Some people embraced the Peace (or should we say embraced each other) with enthusiasm. Others were less convinced about the Peace and never took to it. There is a church in Yorkshire where a notice in big red print is fixed to the minister's stall for the benefit of visiting clergy: 'We do *not* have the Peace in this church and we do *not* shake hands.' But a minister who is deputizing at a church where the congregation loves the Peace may disappoint the people by missing it out, just as much as might happen by trying to include it with a congregation that isn't used to it.

It's not just a matter of a congregation's expectations. The Peace has the potential to be a powerful symbolic act. What does the Peace really mean, and what makes this greeting different from others, such as a welcome at the door?

A holy kiss

Like a number of features that were thought of as being new back in the seventies, introducing the Peace was actually a matter of bringing something with a long history back into use. To set the scene, we need to bear in mind that in the time and culture of the earliest Christians generally a kiss was a normal gesture of greeting, between men as well as between women. Paul writes to the church in Rome, 'Greet one another with a holy kiss' (Rom. 16.16; almost identical words appear at the end of 1 and 2 Cor. and 1 Thess.). Very similar to that are the closing words of 1 Peter: 'Greet one another with a kiss of love. Peace to all of you who are in Christ' (1 Peter 5.14). So not only was a kiss a normal greeting but also there was a special meaning attached to a *holy* kiss, a kiss that was given in the setting of a meeting of people who shared the Christian faith. A second strand linked to the practice of exchanging the Peace at the Eucharist comes from Jesus' words in Matthew 5.23–24: he teaches that it is pointless to offer a sacrifice in the Temple in the hope of putting oneself in a right relationship with God, if there is a human relationship that needs putting right first: '[W]hen you are offering your gift at the altar, if you remember that your brother has something against you, leave your gift there before the altar and go; first be reconciled to your brother'. One of the early texts about Christian worship, Justin Martyr's *First Apology* from about 150, states 'when we have ended the prayers' (that is, before the table is prepared and the bread and wine are offered) 'we greet one another with a kiss' (*First Apology* 65.2). Another very old text, Hippolytus' *Apostolic Tradition*, from the early 200s, also mentions the practice of worshippers greeting each other with a kiss.[20] So we know that the Peace in the Eucharist goes back a very long way; and the position in the Eucharist that Justin mentions will also be familiar to Anglicans and many other Christians today.

---

20 R. C. D. Jasper and G. J. Cuming (eds), 1980, *Prayers of the Eucharist Early and Reformed*, 2nd edn., New York: Oxford University Press, pp. 18–24.

Why did the Peace disappear from Anglican services? It was part of the medieval Latin liturgy, and it did survive in the form of a spoken exchange in the first *Book of Common Prayer* of 1549 ('The peace of the Lorde be alwaye with you; And with thy spirite'). But all the greetings between priest and people were removed in the 1552 Communion service and they were never put back in the later English Prayer Books. So in the Church of England at least, the Peace in any form dropped out of the shared memory for 400 years.

It was in the 1950s that the Peace started to reappear, in the ecumenical Church of South India's form of service which encouraged worshippers (with some carefully worded instructions!) to greet each other with a double-handed clasp. The Church of England's *Series 3* suggested a 'handclasp or similar action'. As the Peace has become a normal part of many forms of celebrating the Eucharist, there is a huge variety in what people actually do at this point of the service (and official service books have give up making specific suggestions). There are hugs and backslaps, kisses, handclasps and handshakes. In some congregations, the custom is to exchange the Peace briefly with the people nearest; among others (especially smaller congregations) everyone greets everyone else individually. The deliberately stylized greeting of the Indian form of service and *Series 3* has to some extent been put aside, which encourages spontaneity, but means that the distinctiveness of the Peace is not signalled quite so clearly as it once was.

While we are thinking about what happens at the Peace, we should not forget that some people are still uncomfortable about it. They may be embarrassed and not feel 'easy' when the Peace is exchanged. The senior generation of worshippers who were brought up (and prepared for Confirmation) before the first batch of revised services arrived, together with the Peace, were often taught that worship was a matter between the individual and God. Confirmation candidates were told to take no notice of who else was in church, and to concentrate on their own spiritual business. And so it is understandable that a number of worshippers still do not feel 'at home' with a practice that, to some extent at least, runs counter to an existing deeply embedded personal pattern of spirituality. And it's important in general to be sensitive and aware of the fact that, for all sorts of reasons, particular individuals might find the Peace (especially with a very hearty and 'space-invading' gesture) unsettling.

Looking at the meaning of the Peace

In general, though, the Peace is an element in worship that most worshippers seem to value and appreciate. If then we are to make the most of it as a symbolic action, it is important that we put good principle and practice together. How and why we 'do the Peace' actually reveals a lot about what we believe and how we put our faith into action.

Being inclusive

First, the Peace needs to be genuinely *inclusive*. If we make a bee-line for the people who are in our close circle of friends at the Peace, and ignore others, we have made the mistake of treating church as a cluster of self-selected friends rather than the family of God. Instead, we must see that here around us are the people that God has given us to worship and work with: not necessarily the people that we would have chosen, or the people that share our interests or that we would choose to spend our free time with. Do we greet newcomers and visitors warmly? Congregations like to think of themselves as friendly and welcoming, and many do try, but the experience of newcomers and enquirers can sometimes be very different as they encounter an unseen barrier. They can themselves feel invisible when people who already know each other well form into 'cells', whether it is at the Peace, at coffee afterwards, or in the life of the congregation generally. So the Peace can be a gesture of welcome, or, perversely, it can both reinforce and symbolize the way that we exclude. It can be surprisingly difficult for newcomers to integrate into an established congregation, to bring new insights, to develop its ethos and enhance its work. Making sure that the Peace is inclusive means that we constantly remind ourselves that life in Christ should change the way we behave towards one another, and welcome new people, new gifts and new opportunities.

Reconciliation

Second, the Peace is about *reconciliation*. Reconciliation is all about a true coming together, and it does not mean being passive and weak. Christians are called to be involved in reconciliation, but that is not the same as giving in to everyone else's point of view. Christians aren't barred from disagreeing or from having sincerely held and different views about all sorts of things. Reconciliation isn't about doing away with those sorts of differences: it is about something much more profound. Christians are called to be agents of reconciliation for Christ's sake. That means recognizing in each person, even someone we find difficult and disagree with strongly, a human being whom God loves and someone for whom Jesus Christ died. It means being open to see the truth in the other person's view, and not letting our anger fester away and turn into something so serious that it alienates us from God (Eph. 4.26).

Church culture is regrettably sometimes better at talking about reconciliation than showing it in action. Even small-scale disputes between individuals show that barriers are easier to build up than break down. The New Testament acknowledges the reality of differences of opinion and of disputes and difficulties that appear within a congregation. It is vital that differences should not poison the life of the Church, cause bitterness and disillusionment, and damage individuals. One set of words that can be used to introduce the Peace is based on Colossians 3.14–15: 'Above all, clothe yourselves with love, which binds everything together in perfect harmony [literally, "is the bond of perfection"]. And let the peace of Christ rule in your hearts, to which indeed you were called in the one body'[21] Christ's peace, Christ's wholeness, is a calling to be members of his body with integrity and love.

Love – in Colossians the word is *agapē*, the same as in Paul's great celebration of love in 1 Corinthians 13 – is not about liking or feeling, emotion or the choice of the moment. Godly love is strong, relentless, reliable and generous. To love someone with this *agapē* is to aspire to value that person as God does and for God's sake. To live in love of that kind is to live in God (1 John 4.16). The Peace is a reminder both that our union in Christ is stronger than our human differences and that it is the basis on which we work towards reconciliation. And to that extent it can be costly. It can be the setting in which people encounter one another – and yes, come close enough to touch – when for whatever reason they have been trying to avoid each other. It can take courage to go to someone at the Peace and hold out a hand, if there has been some offence caused and somehow the right words have not come, or wounds are still raw. The Peace *can* be the discreet first contact that leads to a fuller mending of a relationship. It can be the vital step towards saying, 'Let's try again.'

Respect

The third point is that the Peace is a moment for giving people *notice* and *respect*. In the Peace, we encounter one another as fellow-worshippers, invited to recognize each other as children together of one heavenly Father, to see the image of God in one another. It is too easy for the Peace to be rushed, in the sense that we so often do not actually look at the person with whom we are exchanging it, but we look over their shoulder to the person beyond. The words from our mouth may be 'the peace of the Lord', but our body language is saying, 'Must get on; can't stop'.

---

21 *Common Worship*, p. 326..

Distinctiveness

Last, the Peace is *distinctive*. Even when the early Christians used a familiar gesture of greeting – a kiss – they described it as something special, a *holy* kiss, because it carried extra meaning within the community of believers. It should be the same for us. The Peace is not a time for saying, 'hello', or, 'how do you do', in the same way that we might say it to a friend in the street. When it was suggested that a handclasp rather than a handshake should be used at the Peace, it was an attempt to mark out the Peace as being different from other greetings, and a hint that the cultural and social associations of an everyday greeting, as well as the conventions that might normally stop people greeting each other, do not apply. The principle is that in the Peace we greet each other for Christ and in Christ. Whatever gesture we choose to use, it's important to remember that we are greeting each other first and foremost because we belong to God in Christ, not because we choose to be friends and neighbours.

Peace and the Prayer Book

Is the spirit of all this missing from the *Book of Common Prayer*? While the Peace itself dropped out of the text and actions of the Prayer Book, some of the issues that we have looked at in relation to the Peace are present in the Prayer Book in a different guise. So, although the Prayer Book has no exchange of the Peace, it does have words which are both an invitation and a caution before the confession. 'Ye that do truly and earnestly repent you of your sins, and are in love and charity with your neighbours, and intend to lead a new life … Draw near with faith, and take this holy Sacrament to your comfort'. The assumption, or we could say instruction, is that those who are not 'in love and charity' with their neighbours (with the widest possible meaning, not restricted literally to the neighbours next door!) should amend the situation before coming to Holy Communion. This is in the spirit of 1 John

113

4.20: 'Those who say, "I love God", and hate their brothers, are liars; for those who do not love a brother whom they have seen, cannot love God whom they have not seen.' In fact the rubrics in the Prayer Book go much further, and state that the priest should discourage parishioners who refuse to be reconciled from coming to receive Holy Communion. Clergy today may understandably be wary of enforcing that discipline! – but the point is that the Prayer Book took the effects of what it describes as 'malice and hatred' in the congregation and community seriously. Otherwise, in the absence of a true peace, or at least the determined will to see peace break out, the confession is a sham and Communion is being treated improperly (1 Cor. 11.27–29).

The Lord's peace

So while there are differences between the approaches to peace and reconciliation found in the Prayer Book and more recent forms of service, there is a principle that they have in common. That is that the Church's forms of worship give a prompt, and sometimes an opportunity, for people to recognize and address those situations where true, profound peace is disrupted. It is important not to treat casually, or worse abuse, elements of worship such as confession or the Peace – to go through the form of *words* while avoiding the hard *work* that we are challenged to do in order to live out the gospel with integrity. The Peace, as a symbolic act, carries real meaning: and therefore it is cynical to avoid doing the work of humility and forgiveness and love that has to be done, if the words or the actions are to convey the meaning they are supposed to symbolize. And worst of all is to allow ourselves to pretend that there is no problem to solve, no need to re-establish true peace, when deep down we know that there is.

All these aspects spring from the fact that fundamentally this is the peace *of the Lord*. That kind of peace means far more than the absence of conflict. It mirrors the love between Father, Son and Spirit, and draws us into the life and love of the Trinity. It is the basis for a bond of commitment that is stronger than the tensions that, without Christ's peace, can result in woefully torn relationships and painfully broken people. To let Christ's peace rule is to live according to Christ's law, which we fulfil by bearing one other's burdens (Gal. 6.2). And to value that peace means being able to recognize when that peace and wholeness is threatened; more than that, to take the trouble to empathize and to strive to see when others are distressed, hurt or anxious, when they feel excluded, demeaned or undervalued. Most of all, it is vital to look for signs that someone's relationship with God is hampered because of something that has happened within the context of the Church. Life in the Church context is no different from other aspects of human behaviour, insofar as friction between individuals and groups can occur, even when no one is deliberately acting badly or setting out to hurt.

Of course we are glad to see our friends in church, and of course there is nothing wrong in greeting them warmly in church. Nobody would want to make the Peace into a cold, formal ceremony. But at the same time, peace is Christ's gift, and the Peace in the Eucharist is a distinctive and special act that witnesses to it, and that goes beyond saying hello to those we like. 'Christ is our peace. He has reconciled us to God in one body by the cross. We meet in *his* name and share *his* peace.'

To think about further

Do we manage to recognize the difference between manageable disagreements and dangerous disruptions in our relationships? Can the Peace point to ways to address our call to live 'in Christ'?

13

Praying the Eucharist

*Grant that these gifts of bread and wine may be to us the body
and blood of our Lord Jesus Christ*

When we hold a service of Holy Communion (or 'celebrate
the Eucharist'), the priest stands at the altar or table and
says a long prayer. Why does she or he do that? What is the prayer
for? Where do the words come from? Is this prayer only to do
with the priest, or does it involve the congregation too? How
much do the actual words matter? The prayer has obviously
got a lot to do with the bread and wine that we are going
to share: but some of the words don't seem to refer to the
bread and wine directly, so why is the rest of the prayer
there?

This prayer is called the *eucharistic prayer*, and it stands in
a prime position in every celebration of the Eucharist, between
the preparation of the bread and wine on the table and the
sharing of Holy Communion. There are many different eucharistic prayers (for instance, *Common Worship* Order One has eight
alternatives, and the Church in Wales service has seven), but there
is a 'family resemblance' between them. In this chapter we shall
look at what a eucharistic prayer is, and we'll use one of them,
Common Worship Prayer B, to help us.

Recalling Jesus' supper

The starting point is the New Testament, which includes four
accounts of the supper that Jesus shared with his disciples the
night before he died (1 Cor. 11.23–26; Mark 14.22–25; Matt.

26.26–29; Luke 22.14–20). In their accounts, Paul and Luke record that Jesus told his disciples to 'do this' in remembrance of him. We will look further at what we mean by 'remember' in Chapter 15: the point for the moment is that Christians share the bread and cup of the Eucharist, not only as a commemoration of Jesus but also because we believe that we are following in the line of his disciples, and obeying Jesus' instruction.

The Eucharist in the earliest days

Even before the Gospels and Paul's letters were written — when the message of Jesus was being carried by word of mouth — Jesus' first followers were already sharing an early form of the Eucharist. Paul's words in 1 Corinthians show that the assembly of believers in Corinth was already doing just that. He writes:

> The cup of blessing that we bless, is it not a sharing in the blood of Christ? The bread that we break, is it not a sharing in the body of Christ? Because there is one bread, we who are many are one body, for we all partake of the one bread. (1 Cor. 10.16–17)

The word translated 'sharing' is *koinonia*, which also has the sense of fellowship, participation, and of deeply holding things in common. It is often translated 'communion', but it means more than 'receiving Holy Communion', the specific act of sharing bread and wine as the body and blood of Christ. It links to the whole theme of common life in Christ, which the earliest Christians understood that they were taking part in. Sharing the Eucharist, and proclaiming Christ's death until he comes (1 Cor. 11.26), was a vital and distinctive focus of that common life, which looked forward to the Messiah's feast at the end of time (Luke 22.16, 18) as well as back to the historical events of the night before Jesus died.

An ancient model: Hippolytus

There's evidence to show that the clustering together of many themes, in the context of the eucharistic prayer, has been a feature of Christian worship since the early centuries. One of the documents that has come down to us from the early days of the Church is *The Apostolic Tradition* by Hippolytus of Rome, dating from about 215, including a description of a prayer to be said at the Eucharist. We can guess that the style and content of Hippolytus' prayer are probably typical of the prayers in use at that time, but surviving accounts are rare and it seems to have been common practice for eucharistic prayers to have been at least partly improvised. In this chapter we will bear Hippolytus' prayer particularly in mind, because a number of churches have used it as a pattern for a eucharistic prayer now in current use, and it is in fact the model for Prayer B in *Common Worship*. Many of the features of Hippolytus' prayer have been borrowed very directly into Prayer B, and, as we shall now see, his 1,800-year-old phrases will resonate with a large number of worshippers.

Praying the prayer

The prayer begins with the minister and people greeting and blessing each other:

> The Lord be with you; *And also with you.*[22]
> Lift up your hearts. *We lift them to the Lord.*
> Let us give thanks to the Lord our God. *It is right to give thanks and praise.*

This opening dialogue is not a mere formality, words for words' sake. It sets the scene for what minister and people are to do, with

---

22 Many churches use the alternative 'The Lord is here. *His Spirit is with us.*' But 'The Lord be with you …' follows Hippolytus' original text.

joy and celebration, as members together of the Church. In this threefold exchange between minister and people, first we greet each other in God's name, second we turn our attention to God, and third state our intention to give thanks to God: that is something we should do at all times and in all places, and at this moment now we are going to concentrate on it, and make it our special purpose.

The prayer celebrates what God has done:

> Father, we give you thanks and praise through your beloved Son Jesus Christ, your living Word, through whom you have created all things; who was sent by you in your great goodness to be our Saviour.
>
> By the power of the Holy Spirit he took flesh; as your Son, born of the blessed Virgin, he lived on earth and went about among us; he opened wide his arms for us on the cross; he put an end to death by dying for us; and revealed the resurrection by rising to new life; so he fulfilled your will and won for you a holy people.

Our thanksgiving is concentrated on the gift of God's Son: who he is, what he has done, and how he has gained a holy people for God (an echo of 1 Peter 2.9). The prayer recognizes the unique importance of Christ's death, of course, but it is striking that the thanksgiving is based on Jesus' taking flesh ('incarnation'), his ministry and resurrection, and not only on his death. All of them are encompassed within Jesus Christ's saving work.

Sanctus

The prayer leads into the section which we call the *Sanctus* (from the Latin word for 'holy'). The introduction to this section invites us to praise God 'with angels and archangels, and with all the company of heaven'. That is a cue for us to remember the source of these words in the vision of Isaiah:

> I saw the Lord sitting on a throne, high and lofty; and the hem
> of his robe filled the temple. Seraphs were in attendance above
> him … And one called to another and said: 'Holy, holy, holy
> is the LORD of hosts; the whole earth is full of his glory.' …
> And I said: 'Woe is me! … my eyes have seen the King, the
> LORD of hosts!' (Isa. 6.1–5)

Isaiah's vision is a moment of breaking through the barrier
between earth, that is, the normal range of human experience, and
heaven. It may be helpful if we think of heaven not so much as a
place as a state of *being* and *existence* in which God is encountered
directly. The Jewish tradition has a very strong theme of God being
separate and Other (and Other is part of the meaning of holy):
Jews believed that it was impossible to see the face of God and
survive (Exod. 33.20). So Isaiah's admission (and it seems more
an admission than a claim) that he has seen God in a vision has a
sense of awe about it that we may perhaps miss. The 'holy' of the
seraphs is the song of heaven that never stops (and is referred to
again in Rev. 4.8). Isaiah has heard their song: in the 'holy, holy,
holy' of the Eucharist we are invited – perhaps it would be more
appropriate to say that we dare – to join in as well. By including
Sanctus in the eucharistic prayer, we are reminded that what we are
doing as we celebrate the Eucharist is not to perform a ceremony
that is human in origin and earth-bound in its purpose. It is sometimes said that the Eucharist is a window into heaven. It is
important not to forget that aspect as we repeat the words from
Isaiah 6, reminding us that the Eucharist is partly about our
encounter with God as the awesome Other.

Sanctus is followed by an echo of the greeting which the crowds
gave Jesus when he entered Jerusalem in triumph (Matt. 21.9):
'Blessed is he who comes in the name of the Lord. Hosanna in the
highest.' The cry of 'holy' speaks of the God who cannot be seen;
'Blessed is he who comes' (*Benedictus qui venit*) uses words that
speak of Christ's arrival, long ago in Jerusalem, and are now used
to greet his presence in the Eucharist. It is beyond our powers of

understanding to know *how* he is present, but we remember his promise that 'where two or three are gathered in my name, I am there among them' (Matt. 18.20).

By the power of your Holy Spirit

Now we move to the part of the eucharistic prayer that retells the story of Jesus' last supper. This prayer introduces it:

> [G]rant that by the power of your Holy Spirit,[23] and according to your holy will, these gifts of bread and wine may be to us the body and blood of our Lord Jesus Christ;

Much paper and ink has been used over the centuries, and regrettably bitter arguments fought, over the question of what happens in the Eucharist; specifically, what happens to the bread and wine, and in what sense the bread and wine *are* the body and blood of Christ. This is not the place to try to give an account of all the different ideas that have been put forward, still less to make a judgement between them. Sometimes the question has centred very much on exactly what words are used, but we ought to be able to look beyond the exact formula of words when we think of God's gift of the Eucharist. Christ's promise is more powerful than human thoughts and words. The best answer to the big question of what happens in the Eucharist, and how Christ is truly present, is 'God alone knows'. In the end, what we are celebrating is the presence of Christ in his Church, in the way that accords with God's will. The limits of our human understanding do not alter the great truth: Christ's presence is real and active, and takes whatever form that God gives, by the power of the Holy Spirit.

And so at this point in the prayer comes the retelling of the

---

23 This invocation of the Holy Spirit has the technical name *epiclesis*, which means 'calling'.

story of Jesus' supper. We call to mind the meal Jesus shared on the night he was betrayed, the night before he gave up himself to death.

> [I]n the same night that he was betrayed, [he] took bread and gave you thanks; he broke it and gave it to his disciples, saying: Take, eat; this is my body which is given for you; do this in remembrance of me.
>
> In the same way, after supper he took the cup and gave you thanks; he gave it to them, saying: Drink this, all of you; this is my blood of the new covenant, which is shed for you and for many for the forgiveness of sins. Do this, as often as you drink it, in remembrance of me.

The Gospels (for example Mark 14.12–16) suggest that this was a Passover meal, the meal held once a year that recalls God's rescue of the Israelites from Egypt and is a reminder of the relationship that continues between God and his people. Passover is one of the strongest expressions of Jewish identity, and contains a number of formal actions or ceremonies, blessings and the sharing of a sequence of dishes of food and cups of wine, each with a symbolic meaning. Jesus gives *this* Passover meal an extra meaning. There is a 'new covenant': a new relationship or agreement between God and humanity. Jesus' blood (that is, his self-giving sacrifice) is a central part of what makes that new covenant (a theme we shall pick up again in Chapter 14). And as we celebrate the Eucharist, the bread and wine become what God makes them.

In the company of all the saints

The eucharistic prayer now moves on, linking the past event of Jesus' last supper with what is happening in the Church's celebration now.

> [R]ejoicing in his mighty resurrection and glorious ascen-

sion, and looking for his coming in glory, we celebrate this memorial of our redemption. As we offer you this our sacrifice of praise and thanksgiving, we bring before you this bread and this cup and we thank you for counting us worthy to stand in your presence and serve you.

Send the Holy Spirit on your people, and gather into one in your kingdom all who share this one bread and one cup, so that we, in the company of all the saints, may praise and glorify you for ever ...

Again, there is far more than an earthly dimension to the Eucharist. Three ways or levels of worship are joined together. One is what happens locally, when we are part of a particular congregation in one place on one day. The second is the worship of the whole Church on earth, in every place and time, of which we are a part. The third is that praise which is only fully possible when God is encountered directly: the worship of heaven. The eucharistic prayer draws together the work of God in Christ and the life of Christian worshippers, together and as individuals, through the living power of the Spirit. It draws together things that we know and things that we cannot fully grasp or even begin to understand.

One Eucharist, many meanings

The eucharistic prayer, then, is like a many-coloured window, with light shining through so many ideas and themes of remembering, thanksgiving and looking forward to the ultimate future that is in God's mind; the majesty of God and the closeness of friendship with Jesus. No single celebration of the Eucharist is going to be able to capture them all fully. A simple 'uncluttered' or 'minimalist' celebration of the Eucharist can speak powerfully of some of these themes; so, in a different way, can a celebration that is full of symbolism, ceremonial and music. A celebration where priest and people are gathered around a table or altar – all facing inwards –

may suggest the setting of a meal, a community celebrating Christ in its midst. It may recall very powerfully for us the intimacy of the room where Jesus shared his supper. Alternatively, a celebration where priest and people face an altar which is placed against the east wall of a church creates a sense of worshipping God who is 'Other', beyond our power to imagine or understand ('numinous' worship). It is no bad thing to be reminded from time to time of the different ways of approaching and understanding the Eucharist, and to experience it celebrated in different settings and in different styles, in addition to the pattern that we are used to, to help us appreciate that.

Everyone's prayer

Before we leave the eucharistic prayer, let us remember its last word: Amen. Amen is not simply a word that neatly finishes off a prayer. It means 'Yes, that's right and true!' Most of the words of this prayer are said by the priest who presides at the Eucharist, on behalf of the whole assembly, but that does not mean it is the 'priest's prayer' in an exclusive sense. It is the final Amen said by all that makes this the prayer of the whole community. It is some-times called the Great Amen, and is intended to be a bold affirmation by everyone present of the whole act of thanksgiving, and our offering of ourselves afresh to God as we prepare to be the guests of Christ at his table.

The many themes of a eucharistic prayer

One way of thinking about this prayer, and of why it is important in the Eucharist, is to look at the place it has in the dynamic and the drama of worship. We need an element in worship that will move us on from the earlier part centred on hearing God's word in Scripture to the moment when we share Communion. To put the point in very functional terms, whatever it is that needs to happen to prepare us for that sharing, and whatever needs to happen in relation to the bread and wine that we will share, this prayer is the means of that taking place.

This is, in every sense, a big prayer. It has many facets to it, and because it is connected so strongly to Jesus' death and resurrection, it is connected strongly with all the major themes of the Christian faith. When we pray the eucharistic prayer, we are invoking God the Holy Trinity: the Father to whom we direct the prayer; Christ whom we are remembering; the work of the Holy Spirit. It touches on themes of our discipleship; the Church in all times and all places; death, life and eternity; and of course the bread and wine in front of us. The eucharistic prayer is about a lot more than 'doing something to the bread and wine'. Eucharist is, literally, thanksgiving, and this prayer is one great action of thanks. The story of Jesus' last supper is retold as part of that thanksgiving, and in a sense is the focal point of it. But this prayer thanks God for *all* his love in his dealings with humanity and the whole of creation. We thank God for everything throughout time. We thank him for what he *has* done, supremely in the events of Jesus' life, death and resurrection; for what he is doing *now*, in us and among us; and also for the *future* that he has in store, when (in whatever way he plans) his intentions and purposes come completely to fruition. And as we recount this great 'story of God', we thank him that we are caught up in it. Supremely through Jesus Christ, human and divine, his story becomes ours.

To think about further

Are there some words and phrases in the eucharistic prayer that you find particularly powerful?

See if you can attend a celebration of the Eucharist in an unfamiliar place and style. Does the experience suggest new ideas or insights to you?

14

Taking sin away

Lamb of God

Lamb of God, you take away the sin of the world, have mercy
on us.
Lamb of God, you take away the sin of the world, have mercy
on us.
Lamb of God, you take away the sin of the world, grant us peace.

This prayer to Jesus Christ with the title of Lamb of God has been
used in the Eucharist for well over a thousand years (often referred to
by its Latin title *Agnus Dei*). Why do we call Jesus the Lamb of God?
And what does it mean to say that Jesus takes away the world's sin?

Lamb of God

Our starting point is John's Gospel, which is where the phrase
Lamb of God comes from. In the Gospel's first chapter, we read
that John the Baptist saw Jesus and declared (the Gospel does not
tell us to whom John said it), 'Here is the Lamb of God who takes
away the sin of the world!' (John 1.29) The day after, John sees
Jesus again and says to two of his own disciples, 'Look, here is the
Lamb of God!' John's disciples (one of whom we are told was
Andrew) then begin to follow Jesus; Andrew tells his brother
Simon, 'We have found the Messiah' (John 1.35–41).

Sacrifice

Why does the image of the Lamb appear here, on the lips of John

126

the Baptist? The answer has two parts to it. The first (as so often the case when we try to understand the New Testament) is to do with the background of the Jewish faith and religion. The words and images and thinking that are found in the Old Testament are the foundation for what we read in the New: and that includes this figure of a lamb that is sacrificed. There is something of a cultural gap for us to cross here. Early Christian thought, including the New Testament, took up the theme of sacrifice strongly in relation to Jesus. However, since sacrifice is not part of our familiar experience nowadays, and modern western society is not really used to the idea and the language of animal sacrifice, it is worth spending a little time setting the scene.

Sacrifice, including that of sheep and lambs, is a practice that goes back into the ancient history of Judaism. Judaism was not alone among religions in including sacrifice among its forms of worship. The Jews practised sacrifice for centuries, until the Temple (which by then was the centre for all Jewish worship involving sacrifice) was destroyed in the year 70. In sacrifice, a precious thing — ultimately, the very life itself of a creature – was offered to God.

There is nowhere in the Old Testament that explains exactly how, in a mechanical or cause-and-effect sense, sacrifice 'works'. A worshipper who brought an animal 'victim' to be sacrificed might lay a hand on it, in order to identify with it, and to associate the death of the victim with the worshipper's desire to be freed from guilt. Actually the Old Testament says at least as much about how one should *not* think about how sacrifice works as how one *should*. It warns against any crude idea that sacrifice automatically makes someone right with God. The insight of the true worshipper is encapsulated when he say, 'Do I eat the flesh of bulls, or drink the blood of goats? Offer to God a sacrifice of thanksgiving' (Ps. 50.13–14). 'If I were to give a burnt-offering, you would not be pleased. The sacrifice acceptable to God is a broken spirit' (Ps. 51.16–17). 'Shall I come before him with burnt-offerings, with calves a year old? ... what does the Lord require of you but to do justice, and to love kindness, and to walk humbly with your God?' (Mic. 6.6–8). There is a strong theme that there needs to be a connection between any act of sacrifice and a person's desire and commitment to follow God's ways.

One episode in the Old Testament that very powerfully links the theme of the sacrificial lamb and God supplying the need for one is the story of Abraham and Isaac (Gen. 22.1–14). Abraham is told by God to sacrifice his only son Isaac as a burnt-offering. When they are on the way to make the sacrifice, and they have all the equipment except the victim, Isaac asks Abraham, 'Where is the lamb for a burnt-offering?' 'God himself will provide the lamb for a burnt-offering, my son,' replies Abraham – the irony being that Abraham is ready to sacrifice Isaac, but in the event Isaac is reprieved, as a ram is caught by its horns in a thicket and is sacrificed instead of the boy. Since early times, Christians have seen parallels between the story of Abraham and Isaac and the death of Jesus.

The Passover lamb

Lambs are connected with one of Judaism's major festivals, that is, Passover, which commemorates God taking the Israelites out of Egypt. The book of Exodus tells that, when the Egyptians were about to suffer the death of their firstborn, the Israelites were instructed to put the blood of a slaughtered lamb on their doorposts so that God would 'pass over' them and not destroy them (Ex. 12.1–13). Slaughtering lambs in preparation for the Passover (also called the paschal festival) was an important part of the yearly commemoration.

Sacrifice: from Old to New Testament

Before we leave the subject, we should also note that the image of God's servant as a lamb ready for slaughter features in the great prophetic books, Isaiah (53.7) and Jeremiah (11.19). So there is a whole range of ideas and of understanding that connects with the figure of the lamb, and the practices of sacrifice and slaughter.

The New Testament writers pick up the concept of sacrifice and Passover, reworking and reassembling the imagery to explain what Jesus has achieved, especially in relation to his death. The letter to the Hebrews uses the thought-forms inherited from the Old Testament as a foundation for understanding Jesus' death: '[U]nder the Law almost everything is purified with blood, and without the shedding of blood there is no forgiveness of sins' (Heb. 9.22). The illustration in Hebrews goes on to use the image of Christ as a new kind of high priest who makes a definitive offering once for all: instead of offering sacrifices day after day, as priests traditionally did, he makes a full and perfect sacrifice of himself, and makes the old sacrificial system obsolete (Heb. 10). Examples of other New Testament writers using the same kind of language include the first letter of John: 'the blood of Jesus ... cleanses us from all sin' (1 John 1.7). The first letter of Peter mentions the 'precious blood of Christ, like that of a lamb without defect or blemish' (1 Pet. 1.19). Paul writes that 'we have been justified by his blood' (Rom. 5.9).

Specifically, the significance of Jesus' death taking place at Passover time is not lost. Luke has a unique turn of phrase to point out that Jesus' last supper took place on 'the day of Unleavened Bread, on which the Passover lamb had to be sacrificed' (Luke 22.7). Paul proclaims boldly that Jesus himself is the Passover lamb: 'our paschal lamb, Christ, has been sacrificed' (1 Cor. 5.7). These words express in 'Passover language' the idea that Jesus is the means by which God brings about his great and definitive rescue: Passover has a new meaning because it is now linked with Christ's self-giving in his death, and his victory over death by his resurrection.

These passages all allude to the costliness of a life given in order to achieve a restoration of humanity's relationship with God: and not just any life, but the life of the Son of God himself. Closely allied to language about sacrifice is the concept of ransom or redemption, of paying a price (which again could take the form of a sacrificial offering) in order to being about release. Jesus speaks of giving his life as a ransom for many (Mark 10.45). Paul reminds the Corinthians that they are not their own, for they have been bought with a price (1 Cor. 6.20; 7.23).

The Lamb of God and the Fourth Gospel

We said that there is a twofold reason why John's Gospel states at an early stage that Jesus is the Lamb of God. The second part has to do with the overall message of the Gospel and how John conveys it. In the Gospel, Jesus is given a number of titles: the Word (1.1), the Light of the world (8.12), the Resurrection and life (11.25), the Way, the Truth and the Life (14.6). His last long teaching to his disciples, before he dies, ends with him proclaiming that he has overcome the world (16.33) and on the cross he announces that 'It is finished' (or 'completed': 19.30). After his resurrection he commissions his disciples with the gift of the Holy Spirit and with the authority they need to continue his mission in the world (20.22–23). John's Gospel therefore shows Jesus changing humanity by his presence, fulfilling every need in his own person, including the need for the means to mend the relationship between God and humankind.

John describes Jesus as 'the Lamb of God who takes away the sin of the world'. The idea of offering sacrifice for sin is age-old, but that of a sacrifice that has power to take away sin on this 'global scale' is in effect new. As we have just seen, John's Gospel uses the expression 'the world' a number of times. In John's Gospel, the work of Jesus Christ is shown as infinitely generous and all-encompassing: 'God so loved the world' (3.16). The world is pictured as a single entity, in great need of God. Similarly, John uses the expression 'the *sin* of the world' (singular), which the text used in *Common Worship* copies.[24] The Gospel text steers us

---

24 Other versions of the text used in worship are often plural, 'the *sins* of the world', but that does not quite match the text in the Bible.

towards understanding sin in terms of one great mass of human alienation from God. On that reckoning, *sin* (singular) is something that affects the whole of humanity, a state of crisis that God resolves in the life, death and resurrection of Jesus Christ.

Atonement

So far we have given considerable weight to the theme of sacrifice in the Old Testament and to the way it is borrowed into the New. The language of sacrifice was familiar to the New Testament writers, and it was a natural way for them to explain the death of Jesus in terms that spoke of benefit and not loss, achievement and not failure. Here was the action that had rescued humanity, definitively, once and for all.

That is not, however, the only way in which Christian thinkers have understood what Jesus did, together with the significance not only of his death, but his resurrection too. The word for this is *atonement*, meaning how God and humanity are put 'at one'. The New Testament writers clearly shared the belief that Jesus's death, which happened at one place and time, had an effect that extended far beyond that one place and time. As time went on, there were developments in the way that Christian thinkers addressed the subject of atonement. Briefly and as simply as possible, we shall look at the main strands of thought, beginning with a slightly different approach within the New Testament.

Christ: obedient, suffering for us, victorious

The New Testament writers insist that Christ brings humanity the promise of life. This comes in two ways: he cancels the effects of sin (that is, death), and he overcomes the power and force of death. Paul writes that Christ, who was perfectly obedient to God, has repaired the damage done by the disobedient Adam, and so he has brought free gifts of grace and righteousness and the promise of eternal life (Rom. 5.12–21). He was 'handed over to death for our trespasses and was raised for our justification' (Rom. 4.25). Paul writes that '[f]or our sake [God] made [Jesus Christ] to be sin who knew no sin, so that in him we might become the righteousness of God' (2 Cor. 5.21). It is striking how many times, when Paul is writing about Jesus' death, he couples it with the promise of renewal, restoration and life. The same emphasis comes in Peter's words:

> Christ also suffered for you ... He himself bore our sins in his body on the cross, so that, free from sins, we might live for righteousness; by his wounds you have been healed ... Christ also suffered for sins once for all, the righteous for the un-righteous, in order to bring you to God. (1 Pet. 2.21, 24; 3.18)

In another image, Paul pictures God in conflict with the forces of destruction: the ultimate victory takes place when death is over-come. In this vein, he writes that '[t]he last enemy to be destroyed is death' (1 Cor. 15.26) and that '[d]eath has been swallowed up in victory' (1 Cor. 15.54). The letter to the Hebrews also uses language about the defeat of death. 'Since, therefore, the children share flesh and blood, [Christ] himself likewise shared the same things, so that through death he might destroy the one who has the power of death, that is, the devil, and free those who all their lives were held in slavery by the fear of death' (Heb. 2.14–15).

More approaches to atonement

Over time, Christian thinkers continued to work at developing an understanding of what Jesus had achieved, that is, *theories of atone-ment*. Each of these is capable of helping us to understand an aspect of what Jesus achieved, but it has been argued that each of them also falls short of a full account of the atonement.

One explanation starts from the principle that humanity's sin is an affront to God's justice. Words in the New Testament about Christ 'bearing our sins' mean that he made himself responsible for satisfying that affront, or that he, personally, suffered on the cross the penalty that otherwise all humanity would have paid. The strength of this interpretation is that it emphasizes what Christ, objectively, has achieved. Some thinkers have, however, considered it to be unsatisfactory in that it insists that a reparation or penalty *had* to be paid, to satisfy either a moral principle a or a demand made by God the Father himself. In other words, it paints a picture of Christ as loving and self-giving, but (and this partly depends on how it is presented) it can lapse into portraying God the Father as unyielding or vengeful. And an understanding of atonement based on penalty and release can sometimes get unhelpfully stuck in the language of the lawcourt.

An alternative approach altogether has concentrated on looking at the example of Jesus, and to his love which he shows even to the point of death: his self-sacrifice is the perfect model of generous, sacrificial love, which is so powerful and compelling when we encounter it that it utterly transforms us. All Christians would agree that the love of Christ is to be celebrated with thanksgiving; and the assurance that Jesus has experienced pain and desolation has sustained many people in their darkest times. But a picture of Jesus as an example who dies in God's cause, while not in itself wrong, risks failing to answer the question of how he solves the crisis of human sin and disobedience – in other words, how and why his death is unique, and different from any other act of martyrdom.

Yet another way of thinking picks up the theme of Christ the victor over death. This theory of atonement too places less emphasis on the idea of Christ making a satisfaction for sin through his death, and concentrates more on his role as a champion for humanity in his resurrection. Because he is the Word made flesh, fully human, he does this from within the company of humanity. He is our liberator from ultimate oppression and slavery – the slavery of death – and he leads humanity to our ultimate destiny of life with God. Allied to this so-called '*Christus victor*' theology is the tradition called the 'harrowing of hell'. This pictures Jesus, after his own death, going in search of those who had died, and leading them out from captivity to death. It is based on 1 Peter 3.19 and 4.6: 'he went and made a proclamation to the spirits in prison ... the gospel was proclaimed even to the dead'. This imagery has always been part of the way in which eastern (Orthodox) Christians think of what Jesus Christ has achieved through his death and resurrection. It's the image behind the eleventh-century Easter hymn we know as 'ye choirs of new Jerusalem':

How Judah's Lion burst his chains
and crushed the serpent's head;
and brought with him, from death's domains,
the long-imprisoned dead.

Different facets

The fact that thinkers have produced different theories of atonement suggests that there is no one complete way of understanding what Jesus has done. Trying to comprehend the atonement is like looking at a great and beautiful sculpture: there is no *one* angle from which you can see every side, no *one* view that shows the whole. Different angles reveal different aspects.

But there are some truths that are essential, irrespective of which theory or theories we find most compelling. The first is that all this is the work of a loving God, whose will is for us to be (as another well-known hymn puts it) ransomed, healed, restored, forgiven. The second is that Jesus Christ, the divine Word made flesh, has a place in the working out of God's plans that no one else could fulfil. The third is that real events – Jesus' death and resurrection – are more than *symbols* of what God has done through Jesus, they are the actual *means* by which he has done it.

Let's go back to the words with which we started, from John's Gospel: 'Here is the Lamb of God who takes away the sin of the world!' Words such as those are part image, part explanation.

God's love is not like some machine that we can dismantle and see how the cogs and wheels drive each other round. Different approaches to atonement may speak more eloquently and convincingly to each of us, and perhaps different ones at different times. Embracing Christ's self-giving, and the atonement that he has brought, are at the core of Christian faith, even if our understanding falls short. Paul says more in a few words than many have said in thousands: 'God proves his love for us in that while we were sinners Christ died for us' (Rom. 5.8).

To think about further

Which approaches to atonement do you find most convincing or compelling? Why?

15

Remembering Jesus

Eat and drink in remembrance

Draw near with faith. Receive the body of our Lord Jesus
Christ which he gave for you, and his blood which he shed for
you. Eat and drink in remembrance that he died for you, and
feed on him in your hearts by faith with thanksgiving.

It is often with these words that the priest invites the congregation to receive Holy Communion. The first words, 'draw near',
might suggest at first that this is an elegantly phrased stage
direction: 'Please get ready to stand up, form a queue, and make
your way forward to receive Communion.' But no: the collection
of key words – draw near, receive, remembrance, faith – make it
clear that this is not an ordinary instruction.

Come close

The point about being invited to 'draw near', or come close, is that
it's not just to do with getting up out of a seat or pew, and walking forward to where the ministers are. It's a much bigger idea, for
in the deep past of religious understanding God was believed to be
completely unapproachable (Ex. 19.12). One strand of thinking
in the New Testament takes this image of it being impossible to
come close to God, and radically changes it. In the letter to the
Hebrews especially, we are told that Jesus has bridged the gulf
between the divine and the human. He is pictured as the great
High Priest, taking over the title of the chief official of the Jewish
sacrificial system, but different from every merely human priest.

He has made the offering that only he could make, of his own perfect life. No other offering (says Hebrews) is of value in anything like the same way. What is more, the offering that Jesus has made changes for ever the relationship between God and humanity. The writer puts the point like this: '[S]ince we have confidence to enter the sanctuary by the blood of Jesus ... and since we have a great priest over the house of God, let us approach [or "draw near"] with a true heart in full assurance of faith' (Heb. 10.19–22).[25]

Christian writers and thinkers have applied this idea of Christ the high priest to the Eucharist. It takes us through a drama of celebrating God's presence, through Scripture, prayer, and Holy Communion. 'Draw near with faith' brings us to the stage in worship where we celebrate Christ's presence in the sacrament as we receive the bread and wine as his body and blood.

With faith

'Draw near *with faith*' might seem a rather daunting kind of invitation, because we may be all too aware that our own faith is dim and marred. But these words don't mean we have to be perfect, or are expected to be 'spiritual virtuosos'. God invites us because he loves us, not because we believe 'enough' in him. They don't mean that we are supposed to know all there is to know about Jesus, or that we need to have got our spiritual life neatly sorted out. And having faith doesn't mean that we are immune from having questions and doubts. Christian faith *does* mean seeing Jesus as the person in whom the love and life of God are fully offered to us. In the end, faith is not something that we build or make. It is an opportunity held out to us by God. It is not about being clever or about how much knowledge we have, and it is not about learning facts or being able to recite religious words by

---

25 In this verse the *Authorized Version* uses the words 'let us draw near', which perhaps explains why the phrase 'draw near' has been used in the words of invitation to Communion for a very long time and has been retained in *Common Worship*.

heart. It is about love and trust. It is God's gift, not our achievement.

Remembering

'Remember' is a word we use in different ways. We use it about
things that we can recall at first hand – 'do you remember the first
time we went to France?' We also use it about things that are out
of range of personal memory. 'We will remember them,' we say at
Remembrance time about the people who died in war, including
those who died longer ago than anyone can recall with a personal,
first-hand memory, but whose memory is kept alive through
stories, diaries, memorials and pictures. So there is *personal* remembering, and also *corporate* or community remembering that
doesn't depend on anyone present actually being a surviving
eyewitness.

   Remember and *remembrance* are words that we use a lot in the
church context as well, and especially in the Eucharist. Paul and
the first three Gospels all include an account of the supper that
Jesus shared with his disciples the night before he died. Here is
part of Paul's version of Jesus' words (1 Cor. 11.24-25): 'This is my
body that is for you. Do this *in remembrance* of me ... This cup is
the new covenant in my blood. Do this, as often as you drink it, *in
remembrance* of me' (italics inserted). This thanksgiving and sharing are the actions that are at the core of the Eucharist. The story
of that supper, that one particular occasion, is sometimes called
'the institution of the Eucharist'. The Prayer Book Communion
service says that Christ 'did institute, and in his holy Gospel commanded us to continue, a perpetual memory of that his precious
death, until his coming again' (a reference to 1 Cor. 11.26).

The Road to Emmaus

As well as those accounts of the 'last supper', there are other parts
of the New Testament that can help us think about the Eucharist.

One of them is found only in Luke's Gospel (24. 13–35). Luke tells of an event late on the day when Jesus rose from the dead. Two of Jesus' followers are walking to a village called Emmaus. Jesus joins them but they fail to recognize him. Jesus asks why they are sad, and (still unaware of who it is they are talking to) they tell him that his death had dashed their hopes that he would 'redeem Israel'. In reply, Jesus explains that it was part of God's plan that he must die before he entered into glory. Then, writes Luke, 'When he was at the table with them, he took bread, blessed and broke it, and gave it to them. Then their eyes were opened, and they recognized him; and he vanished from their sight.' The two followers go to Jerusalem to tell the eleven disciples 'how he had been made known to them in the breaking of the bread'.

It is interesting that Luke uses that phrase 'the breaking of the bread' in the Emmaus story. By the time the Gospels were written, 'the breaking of the bread' was being used as a way of describing the Lord's Supper (see, for instance, Acts 2.42). That fact itself, and the way the story is told, suggest that the account of the disciples on the road to Emmaus is as closely connected with the Eucharist as the Last Supper is. We could say that the two stories are a mirror image of each other: the Last Supper points to the relationship with God that comes through Jesus Christ's *death* (the 'covenant in his blood') and the story of the road to Emmaus is about recognizing the risen Christ for who he is, when he has entered his resurrection *life*. Both are set in a scene of bread taken, blessed and broken.

So we too are invited to recognize Jesus in the breaking of the bread; to 'do this in remembrance' of him. 'Remember' does not only mean marking the fact that something has happened in the past. It is not the same as commemorating a historic event such as a war. It's more even than knowing that we are part of a 2,000-year-long line of Christian believers who have handed the tradition of celebrating the Eucharist on from one generation to the next. And there is more meaning in the *remembrance* that happens in the Eucharist than there could be from imagining ourselves, even in the most vivid way possible, as having been *there* 2,000 years ago; more than recreating a scene and repeating these actions; more than keeping a tradition alive.

Jesus among us

This kind of remembrance is not about wishful thinking and longing on our part, a kind of fantasy or daydream. It is not simply about us thinking or imagining what it would have been like to be *there*: rather, it is also about Christ (in reality, not imagination) being *here*. His presence gives the foundation and rationale for this special kind of remembrance. The two-thousand-year time-distance between the Last Supper and today is real, yes: but, by God's grace and through Christ's presence, there is a real sense in which that separation of time means nothing. We are God's partners in this act of remembrance, and the past and the present are fused together.

Looking at the story of the road to Emmaus can help us again here. Mysteriously, it is just at the moment when the disciples recognize Jesus that he vanishes. We can read this account as Luke reassuring us, his readers, that Jesus' resurrection is absolutely and unambiguously real: while at the same time he asks us to acknowledge that, after Jesus' ascension, his later followers cannot have the same experience as the first disciples did of meeting the risen Christ in visible form. The Emmaus story makes a link between the time when Jesus appeared to his friends after his resurrection and the time afterwards (the time we stand in now) when those resurrection appearances have ceased but Christ is still present. Jesus disappears from the Emmaus travellers' sight, but he has not abandoned them, and in a deeper sense he is still with them. And while at first they had thought Jesus was to be their guest, as events unfold, they become his guests instead.

The Invitation to Communion draws us into this creative remembering, and knowing that Christ is present. It reminds us that our faith is grounded in the meals and meetings that Jesus had with his disciples. In the Eucharist we keep the memory of an actual event alive: but there is far more to the Eucharist than recalling the past. To draw near as Christ's guests is to celebrate his presence and to give thanks for everything that God has done, is doing and will do, until human history as we know it comes to an end.

To think about further

Which words in the invitation to communion ('Draw near …') speak to you most powerfully? Why?

To what extent do you find that it is always the same words that resonate with you, or do different words 'speak more clearly' to you on different occasions?

16

Unworthy but accepted

You are the same Lord

There was a lady who was housebound and who used to have Holy Communion brought to her at home. As part of the 'home communion set' there was a card with prayers in big print. 'I don't mind what else you do,' she said, 'but I always want us to use this prayer here.' And she pointed to the prayer we know as the Prayer of Humble Access:

> We do not presume to come to this your table, merciful Lord, trusting in our own righteousness, but in your manifold and great mercies. We are not worthy so much as to gather up the crumbs under your table. But you are the same Lord whose nature is always to have mercy. Grant us therefore, gracious Lord, so to eat the flesh of your dear Son Jesus Christ and to drink his blood, that our sinful bodies may be made clean by his body and our souls washed through his most precious blood, and that we may evermore dwell in him, and he in us.

I suspect that that lady was typical of many Anglicans in her love of this prayer. It is especially interesting, not only because it enshrines so much about spirituality and the Eucharist but also because there are two paradoxes that are bound up with it. The first is that the prayer, much loved as it is, is often misunderstood. And the second is that although it has a firm place in Anglican tradition, it has no fixed place in Anglican liturgy.

Where this prayer came from

While many of the prayers which were used in the first English *Book of Common Prayer* were borrowed from earlier Latin originals, this prayer has a different history. It appeared as one of the newly composed texts that were published before the first complete Prayer Book in 1549. Fascinatingly, it captures the spirit of the Anglicanism of Cranmer's time in a number of ways: first, it is heavily influenced by the Bible; second, it is written in finely crafted English; and third, it reflects the various strands of thought that were current in the 1540s and which developed into mature Anglican theology as we know it.

Not another confession

The reason why this prayer is sometimes misunderstood is that it is thought of as being another confession. Quite some while ago in the service, we said we are sorry and we have been forgiven: why are we doing it all over again? But in fact this prayer is definitely *not* another confession. Nowhere in it do we say that we are sorry, and nowhere do we call to mind our sin. The point of the prayer is different. Look at the last line, which contains the idea to which the prayer is leading. It then becomes clearer that is a prayer that Christ may live in us, and that we may live in him. The sign and the means of that gift and grace is Holy Communion. We pray this prayer as we prepare to receive Christ's life-giving Body and Blood: and in order to receive them in a right spiritual frame of mind, we need to understand that we come as God's guests. We do not deserve what he gives us, and we have no right to make any demands. This prayer is a celebration of God's love and generosity, and an acknowledgement of human need. It is not intended to make us feel wretched, worthless and sorry: it is a prayer of wonder and joy that God invites us to his table. It's a prayer that our lives may be brought into line with what God intends and what he offers. It's a prayer in which we make ourselves open to God, open to be changed by him.

Why does this prayer come in different places?

If you have been to more than one form of Communion service in Anglican churches, you may have noticed that the Prayer of Humble Access appears in different positions during the course of the service. Why and how has that happened? When the prayer was new – that is, in the interim Communion service of 1548,[26] and in the first Prayer Book of 1549 – it was placed just before the time of receiving Holy Communion, as a final prayer of preparation. In the 1552 book it was moved to a position before the consecration prayer, where it stayed in 1662. Some Anglican churches (notably in Scotland and America) have for a long time retained the prayer in its original position, just before Communion. However, when the Church of England produced experimental forms of service in the second half of the twentieth century, the prayer was moved to yet another newly invented place, after the intercessions and before the preparation of the table and the eucharistic prayer, a position it has also in the revised Welsh form of service. The latest English form, *Common Worship* Order One, returns to the pattern of 1549.

Here's our second paradox, then. What is the right place for this prayer? It would be unreasonable to accuse the liturgy writers of not being able to make up their minds. There is a rationale for each of the positions in which this prayer has been

---

26 At the beginning of Edward VI's reign, in 1548, a number of English texts and prayers were officially published. They were to be interpolated in the Latin Mass, as an interim measure, until the first complete English service was authorized the following year. They included the invitation to confession, the confession itself, 'Comfortable Words' and 'Prayer of Humble Access', in a version very like the one which is familiar to us from the 1662 Book.

put,[27] but clearly no universal agreement. When we say the prayer just before Communion, we are admitting even at the last moment that we have no right to come to God's table: the same hesitancy that George Herbert expresses in his poem 'Love bade me welcome'. But perhaps then there *isn't* a single, ideal, 'right' place for this prayer. We *could* say that the spiritual truth that the Prayer of Humble Access is expressing 'floats' over the whole of the celebration of the Eucharist. It's as if this prayer belongs 'nowhere and yet everywhere' in the service. As well as being a prayer of preparation, it is also a prayer that sets out the relationship between God and the people who are coming to his table. It is a prayer that invites us to turn over in our minds a reality that is always true: 'You are the same Lord, whose nature is always to have mercy.'

Mercy

The theme of God's mercy is heavily underlined in the Prayer of Humble Access, and the word comes three times: 'Merciful Lord … manifold and great mercies … whose nature is always to have mercy.' The prayer uses the image of God's table. The theme of a meal or banquet at which God is the host and people are his guests is a well-established one (we can see its ancient origins in the prophetic promise of God providing a banquet in Isaiah 25.6). But there is also another and rather more personal image in the background of the Prayer of Humble Access. The text of the prayer recalls the episode in Jesus' tour around Tyre, during which a woman asked him to free her daughter from a spirit (Mark 7.24–30; Matt. 15.21–28). Jesus gives a reply which

---

27 Briefly, the decision about the most appropriate place for the Prayer of Humble Access depends mainly on the question whether it should be said before or after the consecration. Commentaries on *Common Worship* explain the reasoning in more detail.

may seem to us brusque and rude: 'Let the children be fed first, for it is not fair to take the children's food and throw it to the dogs.' That is, his ministry was to the people of Israel, not to Gentiles (the people of other nations). 'But she answered him, "Sir, even the dogs under the table eat the children's crumbs (Mark 7.27–28)."' Our prayer borrows phrases from this scene to underline how we are in a less-deserving state even than outsiders and the dogs that scavenge what scraps they can. But we are not to despair, and we are not turned away, because of God is patient and generous.

The next section of the prayer is particularly carefully nuanced. We pray 'so to eat' Christ's flesh and drink his blood, that our bodies may be made clean, our souls washed, that we may dwell in Christ and he in us. That little word 'so' is vital to the full sense of the prayer. *How* we receive the sacrament, that is in what frame of mind and what spiritual state, is critical. Cranmer and the English Reformers placed considerable importance on receiving the sacraments in a 'worthy' or 'due' fashion. Here they are explaining this point, in the instructions that were printed with the 1548 collection of prayers. When the priest gives the congregation notice that he is going to 'offer ... the most comfortable [that is, strengthening and reassuring] Sacrament of the Body and Blood of Christ', he is to tell the people how Christ gives us his Body and Blood:

> spiritually to feed and drink upon ... My duty is to exhort you in the mean season to consider the greatness of the thing, and to search and examine your own consciences, and that not lightly, nor after the manner of dissimulers with God [in other words not hiding the truth]; but as they which should come to a most godly and heavenly banquet.

The point that the Reformers emphasized was that the communicant's frame of mind was vitally important, and that Holy Communion has to do with 'digesting [Christ's] death in our minds, as our only price, ransom and redemption'.[28]

Body and soul

The Prayer of Humble Access picks up an image from medieval worship and teaching, 'that our sinful bodies may be made clean by his body, and our souls washed through his most precious blood'. We may think that it is rather crude to imagine that Christ's flesh makes our body clean and his blood washes our souls. The logic of the medieval idea is actually a little more subtle, and it goes like this: blood was understood to be the essence of the life-force (Lev. 17.14), and the soul is life, so (putting those two ideas together) the blood of Christ has a particular affinity with the soul.[29] Conversely, it was thought, his body must therefore have an effect on our bodies. Whatever our view of that medieval line of argument might be, we can be confident that the Reformers did not believe that Christ's flesh *only* had an effect on our bodies and his blood *only* on our souls. It is more helpful to think in terms of 'both-and' rather than 'either-or'. That is, God offers grace to our whole being in Holy Communion.

Dwelling

The prayer comes to its end by asking God to grant that we may receive Holy Communion as he intends, 'and that we may evermore dwell in him, and he in us'. We pray that we may find ourselves in the position of those to whom Jesus says: 'Those who eat my flesh and drink my blood abide in me, and I in them' (John 6.56). There is a special close intimacy in the sacramental action of eating and drinking: the signs of Christ's love enter into our

---

28 J. E. Cox (ed.), 1844, *Writings and Disputations of Thomas Cranmer relative to the Sacrament of the Lord's Supper*, London: Parker Society, p. 264, quoted in Katie Badie, 'The Prayer of Humble Access', http://www.churchsocety.org/churchman/documents/Cman_120_2_Badie.pdf

29 Thomas Aquinas, *Summa Theologica*, 3.74.1.

physical bodies and become part of us. So union with Christ is linked with the ongoing work of God's Spirit. We are to see ourselves as a dwelling-place of God's Spirit (1 Cor. 3.16), open to grow in grace, walking in the footsteps of the first disciples who 'devoted themselves to the apostles' teaching and fellowship, to the breaking of bread and the prayers' (Acts 2.42).

Many people have a special affection for the Prayer of Humble Access, because it has within it the picture of a faithful, loving and constant God who never turns people away when they are ready to accept what he, and he alone, gives: a God whose generosity overcomes not only our failure but also any reluctance we might have. The prayer has found its way deep into the hearts of people who are at home in each and every part of the spectrum of Anglican thinking and spiritual life. At so many levels, it is a remarkable achievement, and a jewel in the Anglican treasury.

To think about further

What are the thoughts and emotions that are most powerful to you as you come to the moment of receiving Holy Communion?

Part 5: Faith and life

17

The Lord's Prayer (i)

Your kingdom come

Millions of times a day, this prayer is said by Christians all over the world:

> Our Father in heaven, hallowed be your name, your kingdom come, your will be done, on earth as in heaven.

When we read and say these words, we are joining in a living tradition of prayer that is special to Christians but which has a very strong Jewish flavour. The idea of God being 'our Father' has its roots in the Old Testament. '[Y]ou, O Lord, are our father; our Redeemer from of old is your name' (Isa. 63.16). 'O Lord, you are our Father; we are the clay, and you are our potter; we are all the work of your hand' (Isa. 64.8). Jesus often speaks of God, and prays to him, as 'Father'. Jesus did not invent 'Father' as a way of addressing God, but it is very characteristic of him: and at the moment when Jesus is praying most intensely, in the Garden of Gethsemane before his arrest, Mark (14.36) makes a point of telling that Jesus used the everyday Aramaic[30] word for Father, *Abba*.

Name

The phrases 'hallowed be your name, your kingdom come, your will be done' are a trio. The pattern and structure of the phrases

---

30 Aramaic is a language similar to the more formal biblical Hebrew. Jesus and his friends would have spoken it day by day.

(even more clearly in Matthew's Greek than our English versions) underline the way in which these words – which touch on God's identity, God's purposes and God's ways – make up a threesome.

Especially in the ancient world, the name of someone or something is thought of as having great meaning and power. A name stands for the whole of whatever or whoever is named. Praying that God's name will be hallowed or held holy means much more than praying that the letters and sounds of God's name itself[31] will be treated with respect (although there is a very strong tradition, to which Exodus 20.7 witnesses, of not literally misusing the name of God). More than that, we are praying that God's name may be honoured, in the sense of everything that God is and everything that God means. We pray that we will truly hold God in awe (which fits the meaning of the word holy or hallowed). 'Hallowed be your name' is a prayer about deep wonder: it is a prayer that we may glimpse and respect the greatness of God.

Kingdom

The second of these phrases contains one of the most extraordinary and powerful expressions in the New Testament. Jesus teaches his friends to pray to God that 'your kingdom' may come. 'The kingdom of heaven' or 'the kingdom of God' is a phrase that comes many times in the New Testament. What are we doing when we pray that God's kingdom may come?

This is a question which has fascinated Christian thinkers through the ages. It brings us up against one of the wonderful yet difficult characteristics of the New Testament. The Bible is not a dictionary or technical manual, and therefore does not give us complete step-by-step definitions of words and phrases. Some-

---

31 In the Old Testament we find a number of names for God, the holiest of which is written in the Hebrew Bible with the letters YHWH. Jews do not try to pronounce this name, and when it occurs in the Scriptures they read instead *Adonai* (Lord). English Bibles translate God's holy name as LORD (usually printed with small capitals).

times the Bible shows us glimpses or different aspects of something dynamic and vital, without giving a full explanation in minute detail. The 'kingdom' that Jesus speaks of is a classic example of this. When Jesus talks about the kingdom of God or of heaven,[32] he often says that it is 'like' something. It is *like* a grain of mustard seed that grows into a big shrub (Mark 4.30–32). It is *like* hidden treasure, a precious pearl, a net catching good and bad fish (Matt. 13.44–50). Jesus does not give a precise definition of the kingdom, but he gives enough of an idea for his friends to know that it brings change and renewal, and that it is challenging and demanding. Sometimes it seems that he speaks of the kingdom as a way of how things will be in the future, promised but as yet unseen: 'I tell you, many will come from east and west and will eat with Abraham and Isaac and Jacob in the kingdom of heaven' (Matt. 8.11). Sometimes it seems that he shows a picture of the kingdom being present in the here and now, and there are times when he seems to mean that the kingdom has come or is near because he himself is present: 'Whenever you enter a town and its people welcome you, eat what is set before you; cure the sick who are there, and say to them, "The kingdom of God has come near to you"' (Luke 10.8–9). 'The kingdom of God is not coming with things that can be observed; nor will they say, "Look, here it is!" or "There it is!" For, in fact, the kingdom of God is among [or within][33] you' (Luke 17.20–21).

This may be a startling kaleidoscope of ideas, and it is probably more important for us to catch the general drift than to try to find a single, tight definition of the 'kingdom'. The point being made is that Jesus' presence in and among humanity, living a human life, is a world-changing event. Jesus calls people to reshape their lives.

---

32 Matthew prefers the expression 'kingdom of heaven' to 'kingdom of God'. This is usually explained as Matthew fitting in with the Jewish custom of guarding against misusing God's name by using an alternative roundabout form of words and not mentioning God directly at all.

33 The Greek word can mean either *among* or *within*.

He invites them to grasp hold of a way of living that is in line with what God intends. And now here is the amazing claim that the Christian faith makes: Jesus is both the messenger of this and in his own person, the message. An example of how the two strands of thought are intertwined is shown in the different gospel accounts of the scene where Jesus enters Jerusalem in triumph. The cries of the crowd are recorded by Mark as 'Blessed is the coming *kingdom*' (11.10) and by Luke as 'Blessed is the coming *king*' (19.38).

Jesus lives his life in the power and conscious presence of God. The kingdom that he preaches means a renewed relationship between God and humanity, God's ways and God's truth fully and finally prevailing, life winning over death. Remember that the New Testament is written in the light of Jesus' resurrection, and the knowledge of that victory inevitably colours and energizes the Gospel accounts of the ministry that Jesus carried out before he died and rose again. The Gospels show Jesus speaking about how things are, or how they will be, according to God's plans and his rule. He invites people to believe and live out the values that are in accord with God's will.

Now and still to come

So when we put all this together, it is no surprise that the theme of the kingdom of God as we find it in the New Testament is too big, too fully overflowing with meaning, for us to say that it belongs *either* to the time of Jesus' earthly ministry *or* to a future we don't yet see. It cannot be locked exclusively into one or the other. This crossing of boundaries between the present and the future is an important principle that runs through the Bible. There is a dynamic blending together of things which are 'now' (things which people experience or see) and things which are 'not yet' (things which are located in a future of God's making). Christians inherited this way of thinking from Judaism, and Christianity sees Jesus as the central figure around whom God's future is to be brought to pass. In Mark's Gospel, Jesus begins his ministry by 'announcing God's good news and saying that the time is fulfilled and the kingdom of God is close: change the way you think and live, and believe in the good news' (Mark 1.14–15; author's translation). 'The time is fulfilled' is a piece of code. It is referring to a theme of expectation and hope that was current in Judaism. We find it in texts outside the body of the 'canonical' Old Testament, for instance, in the book of Tobit, which tells of the hope that God will again have mercy on the scattered and captive inhabitants of Israel, 'and they will rebuild the temple of God, but not like the first one until the period when the *times of fulfilment* shall come' (Tob. 14.5; italics inserted). A crucial theme in the New Testament is that God's purposes are being brought to fruition at just the moment he intends. So it is that Luke shows Jesus seizing the moment at the beginning of his ministry in the scene at the synagogue in Nazareth (Luke 4.16–22). Jesus reads from the book of Isaiah, telling how God's servant will bring God's good news to the poor, proclaim release to captives and recovery of sight to the blind, and freedom for the oppressed: to proclaim the year of the Lord's favour (Isa. 61.1–2). And then Jesus says, 'Today this scripture has been fulfilled in your hearing' (Luke 4.21). The year of the Lord's favour is 'today'. It is here, says Jesus, in your sight and in your hearing: you are witnesses of God at work.

Citizens of the kingdom

'Your kingdom come', then, is a prayer for the coming of God's way of how things must be. One strand of this is the conviction that God will bring his purposes to their ultimate and wonderful fulfilment. But we are called to live as citizens of the kingdom now. The Greek word for kingdom is *basileia*, and in normal language it *can* mean a kingdom or dominion in the sense of a piece of territory. However, *basileia* means something other than territory here. It means kingship, or rule: the state of how things are and how they are governed, rather than a piece of land on a map. 'The kingdom of God' therefore means 'how things are when they happen God's way'. The good news that Jesus brought and taught, and embodied, came into the lived experience of the people that the Gospels tell us about. Jesus' appearance signals 'things happening God's way'. But that doesn't mean that the kingdom, the rule of God, is as yet finally complete, because Jesus' ministry is also a foretaste of a future that is part of God's plan. Meanwhile, therefore, Christians are to live in a state of awareness that our destiny is in the kingdom of God which (Paul writes) is 'righteousness and peace and joy in the Holy Spirit' (Rom. 14.17).

So there are various aspects to the idea of the 'kingdom' that belong together: one centred on Jesus and his presence; a second being the life of the Church in the Spirit, inspired by the teaching and example of Jesus; and a third being the future hope that God will complete all things according to his plan. These are intertwined in the New Testament, and whenever we meet the word 'kingdom' it is probably helpful to think of that blending of meaning – to think of it as a word that encourages us to make connections with the different aspects of the whole theme – rather than try to put the word into a compartment each particular time it occurs, as if to say: 'now it means this, but now it means that'. 'Your kingdom come' is a prayer that Christians have always hoped will be fulfilled in God's final plan and in our ultimate destiny. But it is also a prayer that we should hope to see answered in the life we experience now. We cannot bring about the final perfection of God's rule in the present, because that is for him to do, but equally we should not think of God's rule in terms of an idealized future that is completely separate from, and has no bearing on, everyday life or how things are now. We *can* work, as collaborators with God, to bring what we have been shown of God's ways to bear on the present. It is possible to say *both* that we have our hope set on God's future *and* that what Jesus has done makes life now different. How we see ourselves, why we do what we do, our relationship with God and our ultimate hope – all of these are caught up in the idea of the kingdom that Jesus preached.

Will

In the Lord's Prayer, as soon as we have prayed for the coming of the kingdom, we pray for God's will to be done. 'Kingdom' and 'will' belong together, because the kingdom of God is the setting for God's will to be perfectly done. 'Your will be done' isn't a 'giving-up' kind of prayer, and it is a very long way from being an expression of hopeless surrender. Praying the Lord's Prayer is to ask for the grace and (as it may be) courage to be able to align our will with what God has shown us of himself and his ways. In this prayer we ask that we can be collaborators with God, not mindless drones. The God to whom we offer our own will in his service is the God who equips his people with gifts, fosters a deep mutual care and respect among his people, and encourages them to be strong when difficulties and opposition come (Rom. 12); the God who invites people to have the same mind as the generous, self-giving, God-focused mind of Christ (Phil. 2.5). Even when the phrase 'your will be done' comes again word-for-word in the Garden of Gethsemane (Matt. 26.42), amid Jesus' agonized and troubled prayer, it is very far from defeated, resigned hopelessness.

Heaven

And finally in these opening phrases of the Lord's Prayer, we pray for God's will to be done 'on earth as in heaven'. In many languages the word for 'heaven' and 'sky' are the same, and, yes, there was a time when our spiritual forebears, like others in the ancient world, thought of the sky as the place that belonged to supernatural beings while we mortal humans occupied the earth we could see (and dead people belonged to a realm underground). We have long since moved away from that model of the universe with its series of 'decks'. As was mentioned briefly in Chapter 13, the idea of heaven has to do with direct experience of God, rather than a place or a time. The distinction between earth and heaven is absolutely not the same as the distinction between ground and sky. It is better to see it as the distinction between our present experience of existence where we 'see in a mirror, dimly' and the existence we hope for in God, when 'we will see face to face' (1 Cor. 13.12): but that should not be confused by turning it into a sentimentalized picture of what we imagine happens to people, and where we 'go', when we die. God's name (that is, the fullness of his being) and his kingdom and will are available to be experienced fully 'in heaven': again, it is something that we take on trust and that is beyond our understanding. Our prayer is that what we see and experience now may be touched and lit up by confidence in what we do not yet see. To pray the Lord's Prayer is to ask that we may have a part in hallowing God's name, by making him known and looking for signs of the Spirit at work; and to have a part in bringing the ways, the perspective and the priorities of God's rule to bear on life as it is lived now, individually and in our common life. And, most challenging of all, if we pray that God's will may be done, the place to start is within ourselves.

To think about further

Very often we pray the Lord's Prayer quickly. Try praying it slowly: take each phrase, and turn it over in your mind before you move on to the next. Does this way of praying it change the way that these familiar words speak to you?

18

The Lord's Prayer (ii)

Lead us not into temptation but deliver us from evil

At the end of the Lord's Prayer, we ask to be kept safe from two things:

Lead us not into temptation but deliver us from evil.

Like the rest of the Lord's Prayer, these words come directly from Matthew's Gospel (6.13). Somehow these words seem to make the Lord's Prayer end on a dark or warning note. What is the background to this sombre part of the Lord's Prayer, and what are we actually praying for?

The end-times

In order to appreciate the full force of these phrases, we need to get close to the first-century mind. Part of the setting for all this is an idea that was widespread among the Jewish people of Jesus' time and place, which appeared in different versions, but in outline was this: people expected that God would intervene in the world, and would be championed by one or more 'anointed ones' or Messiahs. There might be a final and decisive event, perhaps a battle, in which a Messiah would lead the forces for good against the forces of evil. In the end, God and all who are on his side would win, and as a result the ways of God would emerge as the future pattern for the world, and evil would be vanquished. The concept of an age of the Messiah (or messianic age) was linked with the idea of the 'time of the end' (from Daniel 11.40) or end-times,[34] a time of crisis, and therefore inevitably of suffering and trouble: 'There shall be a time of anguish, such as has never occurred since nations first came into existence' (Dan. 12.1). That verse from Daniel is quoted in the Gospels (Mark 13.19), along with other similar references. It is clear that the theme of the 'end-times' had a lot of influence on the New Testament, and the Gospels hint that it had a large part in Jesus' thinking and teaching.

After Jesus's death and resurrection, some of his followers seem to have believed that a final decisive event, or God's overturning of human history, or both, would come soon – possibly before the people who were then alive died out (there are hints in passages such as 1 Thess. 4.13–5.11; John 21.20–23; and Rev. 16.14). Clearly no such literal event has occurred, and we already read strong hints in the New Testament that it is pointless or wrong to speculate about the timing of events that God has planned (Jesus' warning to his disciples to be alert, because only the Father knows about 'that day or hour', Mark 13.32, and his parting words to his disciples in Acts 1.7, for instance). But irrespective of timescales, Jesus' followers believed that his appearance as Messiah, and his death, resurrection and ascension, signalled the beginning of a new phase of history. Part of the implication of all this is that the followers of the Messiah must expect not only to live through times of difficulty and testing, but must also to suffer opposition and persecution. So they must not be surprised when this happens, and when it does they are encouraged to stay confident in God and faithful to him (Mark 13.7–13; John 15.18–27).

Testing and evil

Another aspect of this prayer has to do with the meaning of 'temptation' and 'evil'. The way we use these words, certainly in

---

34 The Greek for 'end' is *eschaton*. A word derived from it, eschatological, is often used to mean 'referring to the end-times'.

a non-religious context, does not quite match the meaning they would have had for Jesus' first followers. The word translated 'temptation' is *peirasmos*, which is associated with putting some-one or some-thing on trial or test. When Jesus is on the point of being arrested in the Garden of Gethsemane, he tells his disciples: 'Keep awake and pray that you may not enter into *peirasmos*' (Mark 14.38). In one of the visionary letters to churches in the book of Revelation, believers are given this reassurance: 'Because you have kept my word of patient endurance, I will keep you from the hour of trial (*peirasmos*) that is coming on the whole world to test [a related word, *peirasai*] the inhabitants of the earth' (Rev. 3.10). Such a trial, then, is pressing, urgent, decisive and danger-ous. Believers will either remain faithful through this trial, and be among those who 'have kept my word and have not denied my name' (Rev. 3.8), or they will be overcome by the weight of opposition.

The phrase translated 'deliver us from evil' is actually am-biguous in the Greek, because it could just as well mean 'protect us from the evil one'. It is a prayer not only to be protected from evil and harm but also not to fall into the clutches of personalized evil which might have power to draw us away from God.

Christian believers take different views about the figure of the devil or Satan, a name that means Adversary. For our purposes now we will simply mention that range of views briefly. The figure of Satan, as a spirit who puts people to the test and brings trouble and woe, originates in the Old Testament (for example, Job 1.6–12; 1 Chron. 21.1). Satan's character develops as the spirit-being who is opposed to God.

Some Christians believe that the fact the Bible mentions Satan settles the matter: he must exist as a personal spirit-being who co-ordinates evil, is still engaged in battle with God and does everything he can to snare people and destroy the ongoing work of the gospel. So, some will say that the only way to explain the extent of evil in the world is to believe that there is a being who has taken the role of Adversary.

Others take a different view: they would say that the figure of Satan is a personification of evil, but it is not necessary to believe in him as an actual, intelligent, really existing being. Each view is open to question, or we could say either view needs to be treated with some caution. The first can fall into something called dualism, which is a word for picturing God and Satan, or Jesus and Satan, fighting for control of the world. To put it crudely, that is to give Satan more credence than he deserves. The second view can fall into the opposite trap, of underplaying the seriousness and force of evil, and of everything that works contrary to God and the gospel. For our purposes now, and whatever our view about Satan as a real entity might be, the point is to recognize that evil and trial, *peirasmos*, are things of enormous and real significance and danger. They involve people in real difficulty and suffering. Some Christian believers may find it difficult to identify with language that hints at a conflict with evil or a demonic force, or may shy away from anything that hints at dualism. Be that as it may, we stand in the spiritual lineage of the first Christians who knew that in Jesus Christ they had had contact with the power of ultimate good, and they had tasted God's promises. It would have been no surprise to them that by being in such close touch with ultimate good, they were likely to feel all the more keenly the force and effects of opposition to it.

The temptation of Jesus

These themes of being under trial and of evil come in various places in the New Testament. *The* stories of temptation above all others are of course the Gospel accounts of Jesus being tested, under trial, at the beginning of his ministry (Matt. 4.1–11 and Luke 4.1–13). The devil appears, whom Jesus addresses by name as Satan (Matt. 4.10). He incites Jesus to show (or is he asking Jesus to prove to himself?) that he is God's Son, by making stones into bread and by throwing himself off a pinnacle of the Temple in the assurance that he would be caught by angels (a reference to Ps.

91.12). The devil promises Jesus worldly glory and power if only Jesus will worship him. Jesus refuses all of these. To have conceded any of them would have been to deny what we might call 'the God-ness of God' – it is God who feeds his people with his word (his creative power) as well as bread (Deut. 8.3); it is wrong to put God to the test in order to make sure he is still there, because that is to wreck any basis of trust (Deut. 6.16); and to put anyone or anything else in the place of God is to deny him and fracture the relationship that should exist between people and God (Deut. 6.13). This episode in the Gospels is not simply about Jesus making good or bad moral decisions, choosing whether to 'magic up' some bread to stave off hunger. It is about something more fundamental. This testing of Jesus reaches to the root of his calling as God's Son, and how in his deepest response to that calling he witnessed to the truth about God himself. In the same way, temptation or testing for people who take faith seriously reaches beyond the often relatively superficial questions about whether to do a 'good' or 'bad' thing. 'Temptation' is about whether people retain their integrity and remain faithful to their calling as God's people and Jesus' followers.

Temptation, trial and being a person of faith

Now it is possible that we may find ourselves in a situation where a decision we take really *does* have to do with our integrity and whether we have the spiritual resources to withstand a course of action that would be tantamount to denying our discipleship. Let us remember, first, that Jesus' trial is about the 'big question' of being faithful to his calling; and, second, that the New Testament pictures *peirasmos* for Christians in terms of the difficulty of remaining true to their identity in the face of serous opposition. Whatever trial, *peirasmos*, means for us, we need to see it as something that bears on the deep level of our Christian calling.

So we pray 'lead us not into temptation' – or, we could say, do not bring us into a situation where our Christian integrity is put to the test. And the fact that this prayer is included in the Lord's Prayer is a reminder that this testing can come at any time, today or in the further future. We don't know.

This theme occurs in the parable of the sower. In Luke's version (8.4–15), Jesus warns that superficial believers, people who are like plants without roots, fall away in the crucial time of trial (in Luke's Greek, the original expression is the *kairos*, or critical moment, of *peirasmos*: 8.13). And when Paul writes to the Corinthians, he encourages them not to fail when they are encountering opposition, because '[n]o testing [*peirasmos* again] has overtaken you that is not common to everyone. God is faithful, and he will not let you be tested beyond your strength, but with the testing he will also provide the way out so that you may be able to endure it' (1 Cor. 10.11–13 (13)). The danger of falling away, failing, when trials of various kinds come was clearly pressing in the early Church (difficulties and persecutions came in different forms) and there seems to have been anxiety lest the trials were too severe to bear. There is a similar tone in Hebrews 2.18: because Christ himself 'was tested by what he suffered, he is able to help those who are being tested'.

Facing difficulties as followers of Jesus

Jesus teaches the people this prayer about temptation and evil in the context of a world that is different from ours, and to a large extent our religious outlook and scientific understanding are different from those of people 2,000 years ago. What do we do then with the prayer and the concepts that are implicit in it?

Some things haven't changed completely. Trial and testing, in the form of opposition and persecution, have faced Christians in many places and throughout history. We should keep those that do face such difficulties now in our prayers, and remember how Archbishop Desmond Tutu described the love and prayers of people in other nations as 'like a wall of fire' around the South African Church when it was encountering its greatest challenges.

At the same time, there is a kind of trial that affects us closer at hand: not deserving the name persecution, admittedly, but a situation that has the potential to make discipleship more difficult, to make it harder or less comfortable to own the name of Christian publicly – at home, at work, at school or college, in political life or in business. One obvious example is to do with the conflict of motives for a Christian engaged in business, commerce and investment: policies that are in line with Christian integrity (sometimes called 'ethical' policies) can be at variance with practices that are designed to maximize profits. There is a host of circumstances in which it might be 'easier', less embarrassing, more career enhancing, not to bear the name of Christian – or, if one *does* bear the name of Christian, to put faith and its implications in a private and personal compartment and to leave parts of one's life and work relatively untouched by it.

For many men, women and young people, addressing this tension is costly and difficult. It is too easy to confuse Christianity with harmless niceness, or maybe a loose idea of decency and fairness that makes no demands in terms of belief, and has nothing of the urgency and energy that marked Jesus' own work and mission. And it is not unknown for it to be said that religion must, in every respect, be a private matter, and that it is the Church's task only to prepare people for the afterlife: it should keep its nose out of 'real' questions in the 'real' world. But that is to make a false distinction, and we should learn from the pattern of the New Testament where the call to place our ultimate hope 'in Christ' is set alongside the call to live amid the everyday in a way that witnesses to being 'in Christ' now. It does no good if Christianity is reduced to blandness, in order to avoid any difficulty in relation to what being Christian means, and what the challenging aspects of the gospel message consist of. But the decision not to take the easy path can come at a price.

To return to an earlier point: the test that Jesus encountered was about whether to follow his calling and be true to God as God really is, or to turn away from both calling and truth. The New

Testament portrays this as a contest of wills between Jesus and Satan: we must take the call to maintain integrity and truth seriously for ourselves, irrespective of whatever view we take about the personal existence of an Adversary-spirit. We need to see the common thread between Jesus' trial and the experience of his followers: how to stay true to what God calls him and us to be; whether it is possible to continue to recognize and acknowledge God as God amid competing (albeit ultimately false) possibilities; and whether our relationship with God is built on trust. How people handle particular ethical choices will relate to whether they are maintaining integrity in their relationship with God: but testing, *peirasmos*, reaches deeper into the matter of sustaining discipleship and of response to God's call than the relatively trivial level to which 'temptation' is often taken as applying. As we pray 'deliver us from evil', we acknowledge the seriousness with which everything that denies and opposes the ways of God needs to be taken – and we recognize that God alone is the source of whatever it is we need to stay true to him, maintain our integrity in faith, and recognize evil for what it is.

To think about further

What do you consider to be the factors and forces that make Christian discipleship difficult? Are you aware of people who experience a conflict of motives and interests, between faith and the other pressures that life brings? How can they be supported and sustained?

19

Being members of Christ's body

We most heartily thank thee

Both the *Book of Common Prayer* and *Common Worship* include prayers to be said after Communion, sounding a note of thanksgiving. In this chapter and the next, we look at one prayer from each book, each distinctively different and each connecting with important themes: about what it means to be God's people, inspired through worship and doing his work in the world.

It is sometimes said that the *Book of Common Prayer* service of Holy Communion is rather short on joy. If evidence were ever needed to the contrary, this prayer after Communion is it:

Almighty and ever-living God, we most heartily thank thee, for that thou dost vouchsafe to feed us, who have duly received these holy mysteries, with the spiritual food of the most precious Body and Blood of thy Son our Saviour Jesus Christ; and dost assure us thereby of thy favour and goodness towards us; and that we are very members incorporate in the mystical body of thy Son, which is the blessed company of all faithful people; and are also heirs through hope of thy everlasting kingdom, by the merits of the most precious death and passion of thy dear Son. And we most humbly beseech thee, O heavenly Father, so to assist us with thy grace, that we may continue in that holy fellowship, and do all such good works as thou hast prepared for us to walk in; through Jesus Christ our Lord, to whom, with thee and the Holy Ghost, be all honour and glory, world without end.

This is a wonderful cascade of celebration for the gift of Holy Communion, with wave after wave of thanksgiving for all that God has given us in the Eucharist, and for all the things of which he has 'assured us'. This is a prayer of confidence that God has given us what we need to be true and effective members of Christ's body, the Church. It celebrates the gift of 'spiritual food' – an echo of Jesus' words,

> [U]nless you eat the flesh of the Son of Man and drink his blood, you have no life in you ... It is the spirit that gives life; the flesh is useless. The words that I have spoken to you are spirit and life. (John 6.53, 63)

When we receive the Body and Blood of Christ in the Eucharist with faith, we are not performing a bare memorial ceremony: but we are taking into ourselves God's life-giving gift and promise, which he offers us through his love. In his 'favour and goodness', God welcomes us at his table.

Members incorporate

In this prayer we thank God that 'we are very members incorporate in the mystical body of thy Son'. In plain language, we are thanking God that we are part of the Church: not the Church pictured as a human organization, but the living organism which gets its identity from Christ himself. The image of the Church as the body of Christ is an important one in the New Testament. It comes in 1 Corinthians 12.27, 'you are the body of Christ and individually members of it', as part of a passage that reminds Christians that they balance and complement each other as servants of God together. The first chapter of the letter to the Colossians describes Christ as 'the head of the body, the church' (Col. 1.18), and the Church as his body (1.24). There is a similar train of thought in the letter to the Ephesians:

[S]peaking the truth in love, we must grow up in every way into him who is the head, into Christ, from whom the whole body, joined and knitted together by every ligament with which it is equipped, as each part is working properly, promotes the body's growth in building itself up in love. (Eph. 4.15–16)

What does it mean for us to think of the Church, and of being its members, in this context? First, the Church is centred on Jesus Christ alone, and therefore the power that unites us is stronger than anything that divides us – which among other things means that we need to keep our differences and disputes in perspective. Second, the Church is what God makes it. It is far more than a human association of people who happen to be like-minded or enjoy spending time together. The phrase in the prayer 'mystical body' means that the body of Christ is a spiritual reality: it is more profound and greater than the organization that we see, the 'institutional Church'. The word mystical means something that does not have a human origin, and that we only understand insofar as God reveals the reality to us. And third, life in the Church is lived together and mutually. We belong to each other, and the Church can only do its work on earth precisely because it is composed of people who are different, and who bring a range of God-given gifts and abilities (Rom. 12.3–8; 1 Cor. 12.4–30).

Heirs through hope

The phrase in this prayer, 'heirs through hope of thy everlasting kingdom', is one of the greatest expressions to be found in the Prayer Book. Paul describes those 'who are led by the Spirit of God' as 'children of God … joint heirs with Christ – if, in fact, we suffer with him so that we may also be glorified with him' (Rom. 8.14, 16–17). Being heirs of a promise together, he writes, breaks down distinctions between Jews and Gentiles, who now share a new identity in Christ: 'the Gentiles have become fellow-heirs, members of the same body, and sharers in the promise in Christ

Jesus through the gospel' (Eph. 3.6). 'Hope' in the Bible and in the prayer does not mean wishful thinking. It means that the inheritance of God's kingdom is a sure and certain promise. It is guaranteed; it is a reality because it is part of God's plan. The fact that it lies in the future for us, and that we have not yet seen it, does not make it any less real or certain.

This takes us into the realm of what the Bible says about the future destiny of the world and humanity. This is one of a number of areas where we find a host of different nuances, shades of meaning, images and emphases even within the New Testament. Analysing and interpreting what the New Testament writers understood and wished to convey about these topics is a huge task in its own right.[35] There is a wealth of themes that includes resurrection, judgement and vindication, glory, feasting and worship.

So it is that Jesus quotes the one clear reference to resurrection in the Old Testament (Dan. 12.1–3), which promises 'those who are wise shall shine like the brightness of the sky' (3), when he describes 'the end of the age' and the kingdom of heaven (Matt. 13.43). He speaks of a banquet in God's kingdom (Matt. 8.11; Luke 22.15–18) and of the 'Son of Man' coming in judgement and glory (Matt. 25.31-46; 26.64).

The event of Jesus' resurrection – when he took on that 'body of his glory' (Phil. 3.21) – is the spring from which our hope of resurrection flows. It is the background to Paul's words as he looks forward to Christ's appearing again: 'our citizenship is in heaven, and it is from there that we are expecting a Saviour, the Lord Jesus Christ. He will transform the body of our humiliation so that it may be conformed to the body of his glory' (Phil. 3.20–21). And he writes to the Corinthians that

If for this life only we have hoped in Christ, we are of all

---

35 See N. T. Wright, 2003, *The Resurrection of the Son of God*, London: SPCK, especially Chapters 9 and 10.

people most to be pitied. But in fact Christ has been raised from the dead, the first fruits of those who have died ... When this perishable body puts on imperishability, and this mortal body puts on immortality, then the saying that is written will be fulfilled: Death has been swallowed up in victory'. (1 Cor. 15.19–20, 54)

The letters of Peter and John contain a similar message of 'revealing':

Blessed be the God and Father of our Lord Jesus Christ! By his great mercy he has given us a new birth into a living hope through the resurrection of Jesus Christ from the dead, and into an inheritance that is imperishable, undefiled, and unfading, kept in heaven for you, who are being protected by the power of God through faith for a salvation ready to be revealed in the last time. (1 Pet. 1.3–5)

[W]e are God's children now; what we will be has not yet been revealed. What we do know is this: when he is revealed, we will be like him, for we will see him as he is. And all who have this hope in him purify themselves, just as he is pure. (1 John 3.2–3)[36]

What about this interim period in which we live? There is a passage in the letter to the Romans where Paul is discussing salvation and our future hope. '[I]n hope we were saved,' he writes: 'Now hope that is seen is not hope' (Rom. 8.24). Paul's words are rather enigmatic but we can paraphrase what he says on these lines: 'Being saved is a matter of living with God's assurance about the future, the details of which we have to take on trust.' So, 'if we are

---

36 For a much fuller and easily readable discussion of the passages in the New Testament about resurrection, see Paula Gooder, 2009, *This Risen Existence*, Norwich: Canterbury Press.

hoping for something that we do not see, then we wait for it with patience' (Rom 8.25). Part of that 'patience' is living with the fact that from our mortal human perspective we aren't yet able to understand what it will be like to experience God's ultimate intentions for us. But that need not stop us from having confidence in it. The climax of what Paul has to say is the key: not even death can separate us from the love of God in Christ (Rom. 8.38–39).

All this pushes the boundaries, both of language and our capacity to understand. Our mental images may need to be kept in check too. For example, 'eternal (or everlasting) life' is a favourite expression found in English versions of John's Gospel, but we should be cautious about how we read this phrase and others like it. The Greek words, *zōē aiōnios*, mean literally 'life of the age', and we are reading something into them that John probably did not intend if we have a concept of 'everlasting' that imagines an infinite succession of minutes, hours and days.[37]

Present and future

Let us return to the text of the prayer. One of the reasons why its imagery is so powerful is that it connects both with the world as we know it and whatever it is that God *does* intend in his 'everlasting kingdom'. The two are bound together, in God's love and in his plans, and through the resurrection of Jesus Christ. It's when the prayer has mentioned three key elements – Holy Communion, the Church and God's kingdom – that we pray that we may 'continue in that holy fellowship' by God's grace, and do the good works he has prepared for us to do.

Life moves on

'Disciple' means 'learner', and to be a disciple therefore means

---

37 Compare 'the life of the world to come' in the Nicene Creed.

never ceasing to learn. 'Life-long learning' has become the norm in society at large, and it is a principle that we can embrace in a faith context too. Life-long discipleship means addressing the question of faith as life goes on and our roles change: for example, what it means to be a person of faith while at the same time being a student, a person building a career, a parent, a leading member of our profession, or a retired person; what it means to be a learning Christian when we feel physical or mental powers reducing with age, and address the prospect of dying. Amid all the other things that continuing in God's fellowship may mean, it must mean that our faith grows and matures in us and with us, and meets the changing situations that our life brings. Receiving what God offers us in Christ with simplicity and trust remains vital, of course ('receiving the kingdom of God as a little child', in the words of Mark 10.15): but we do not, and cannot, stay children. We must give room for our faith to address the concerns that are appropriate for each of our life-stages. So we need to think of 'continuing in God's fellowship' far more creatively than praying that we can stay still in some sort of 'steady state'. That really isn't possible or healthy.

The Church moves on

What is true for us as individuals is also true of the Church as a body. The Christian faith says that some things are constant: among them, humanity's need for God, and God's love that fills that need. Some truths are constant, for example, the truth about who Jesus is. Some things associated with faith have stood the test of time: one of them is the *Book of Common Prayer* itself, the words of which have power to move and inspire, to teach and comfort, almost 500 years since its first version appeared. But there are many things about the Church and how it functions – its structures and culture, and much of the *style* of activities, worship, music and words – that don't *have* to stay the way they are, as there is only one possible way of outwardly expressing the Christian faith.

Albeit with good intentions, Christians have often slipped into equating an encounter with Jesus Christ and being inspired by the gospel with being drawn into church culture. Even if our motives are good, if the way we live out the life of faith turns out to be shaped around our *own* culture and preferences, our own lifestyle, and a specific idea of how things 'ought to be done', there are real questions about how clearly we are honouring the principle of being a holy company shaped according to *God*'s will. So it is important to have a big vision of what the holy company is that God may be calling his Church to be. Our model of Church must not only be one that looks outwards rather than in but also one that is prepared to see the life of the Church responding to the needs of mission.

Being Church: Fresh Expressions

The twenty-first century is an exciting as well as difficult time for the organized Church. Inherited modes of Church are still important and still have much to offer: they offer stability, beauty, the centuries-old accumulation of experience, and at their best they offer love and communicate genuine Christlike, Christ-centred good news and a long-standing visible presence in a community. After all, the premise on which this book is written is that the words of inherited modes of liturgical worship have the potential to be a springboard for our thinking, praying and learning. But venturing beyond the bounds of inherited modes is vital if, in some places at least, the visible Church is not to confine itself to a membership consisting of people who share the same tastes in music and words, and who like the same kinds of worship and church-based social activity – and, dare one say, might all be of a similar age and social profile.

An important part of what the Church is doing to explore these issues, and re-examine assumptions, goes by the general name of Fresh Expressions. Fresh Expressions – defined as 'a form of church for our changing culture, established primarily for the benefit of people who are not yet members of any church'[38] – may look, sound and feel very different from inherited modes of church life and worship. And (here is the challenging shift in thinking) Fresh Expressions have their own integrity 'as Church', and it is a mistake to see them as intended only for a shifting population of new or young worshippers. Fresh Expressions do not exist to give people a taste of Christianity on their way to 'real' or inherited Church. It may or may not be a practical proposition for a Fresh Expression to take root in any community – an effective Fresh Expression typically needs to be properly resourced and planned – but the website contains many encouraging examples of what has been tried elsewhere. There are Fresh Expressions in urban, suburban and rural settings, and across the spectrum of theological outlook ('churchmanship'). Even if you aren't contemplating a Fresh Expression, it's an inspiration to see that the gospel is alive in a host of unexpected and innovative ways.

I have deliberately included a few words about Fresh Expressions in a chapter based on the Prayer Book, partly because 'Prayer Book people' are often more confident and positive about new ventures than they are given credit for; and partly because new ventures do not detract from the inherited Church and what it stands for, any more than the composition of a new play or symphony is a threat to the standing of Shakespeare or Beethoven.

Walking where God has prepared for us

As the prayer draws to its close, we ask God that we may 'do all such good works as thou hast prepared for us to walk in'. We are praying that we may be able to say our Amen to God's actions, and express what we are by his gift and grace, in our own actions. There is something fascinating about the way in which this prayer

---

38 See www.freshexpressions.org.uk

suggests that God, who has planned his dealings with humanity from all eternity, has fitted into his plan the opportunities for 'good works' to be done by us. To walk in good works may seem a slightly odd phrase, but it picks up the idea that the law of God is a way in which one walks (Psalm 119.1), and again there is a progressive journeying through life. 'Doing good deeds' does not *make* a person a Christian: rather, a faith that is alive is the springboard from which to see that God's 'service is perfect freedom'.[39]

Being the Church

We have seen connections between this prayer and a number of aspects of what it is to be the Church of Jesus Christ. It is united in and around him. It is what God makes it, and it is his, not ours. The Church isn't in its nature culturally narrow. We are called to walk where God sends us and to be confident about new ventures in the gospel. It is in the nature of the Church to be united, to be conscious of belonging to God, present through place, time and eternity, and focused in mission: or, to use the words of the Creed that touch on these themes, *one, holy, catholic and apostolic*. And the centuries-old words of this prayer of thanksgiving for Communion binds together our prayer and commitment to being part of the mission of God's Church in this world, with the hope that he gives us in Christ for whatever lies beyond it.

To think about further

How is it possible to combine respect for tradition with a forward-looking commitment to mission and evangelism?

---

39 From the second collect at morning prayer in the *Book of Common Prayer*.

20

Thanks, praise and discipleship

Live his risen life

In this chapter, we are using a prayer that first appeared in *Series 3* and the *Alternative Service Book* as a text for the priest to say alone. But congregations got into the habit of saying it together, and now in *Common Worship* it has been 'adopted' as a prayer for everyone to say together.

> Father of all, we give you thanks and praise, that when we were still far off you met us in your Son and brought us home. Dying and living, he declared your love, gave us grace, and opened the gate of glory. May we who share Christ's body live his risen life; we who drink his cup bring life to others; we whom the Spirit lights give light to the world. Keep us firm in the hope you have set before us, so we and all your children shall be free, and the whole earth live to praise your name; through Christ our Lord.

This is a prayer of thanksgiving, but it is more. It starts with a celebration of God's love in Christ. That striking phrase 'when we were still far off you met us in your Son and brought us home' is a sideways look at a passage from the Bible. It echoes the parable Jesus told of the prodigal son (Luke 15.11–32). A young man leaves home and squanders an advance on his inheritance. He comes to his senses, and journeys back: 'But while he was still far off, his father saw him and was filled with compassion; he ran and put his arms around him and kissed him (20)'. The father doesn't sit at home watching the figure on the horizon come near: he runs

177

to meet him. He interrupts the fine words of the boy's rehearsed apology with a spontaneous physical gesture. The father in the parable stands for God: it tells how God's love envelops us when we come to him, how it is strong enough to feel around us, immediate enough to seize the opportunity, to delight and to surprise.

It slightly changes the imagery of the parable to pray 'you met us in your Son', but the point is still clear. The outgoing love of God in Christ 'brings us home': it escorts us back to where we should be, from a situation marked by failure and despair. Most important of all, there is no 'I told you so' lecture. God's forgiveness enables a fresh start. It accepts and restores the person who has been wayward and lost, without humiliation. We are able to experience the reconciling love of Christ both 'dying and living':

> God proves his love for us in that while we still were sinners Christ died for us … if while we were enemies, we were reconciled to God through the death of his Son, much more surely, having been reconciled, will we be saved by his life. (Rom. 5.8, 10)

Grace

The prayer goes on to say that God has given us grace. In everyday speech 'grace' usually has something to do with 'looking good' or 'moving gracefully'. Or, it can mean 'doing something with a good grace', when someone overcomes a sense of reluctance or disappointment. In the New Testament, 'grace', *charis*, has a different meaning, centred on God's strong loving kindness. It refers to the goodness of God's plan for humankind: God saved and called us

> not according to our works but according to his own purpose and grace. This grace was given to us in Christ Jesus before the ages began, but it has now been revealed through the appearing of our Saviour Christ Jesus, who abolished

death and brought life and immortality to light through the gospel. (2 Tim. 1.9–10)

Charis is used to describe the generosity of Christ in setting aside divine 'riches' to become poor for humanity's sake, 'so that by his poverty you might become rich', and might in turn be inspired to make a response of generosity (2 Cor. 8.7–9). Grace is what God gives in order to cancel the alienation of sin, and it sustains our life in him (Rom. 5.20; 6.14; Eph. 2.5). 'Continuing in the grace of God' is practically another way of saying 'continue to be faithful as a Christian' (Acts 13.43); and grace is the 'umbrella' term that Paul uses in connection with the variety of gifts that equip the Church for its mission (Rom. 12.6). It enables integrity in ministry and discipleship: 'we have behaved in the world with frankness and godly sincerity, not by earthly wisdom but by the grace of God' (2 Cor. 1.12). The Word lived among us 'full of grace and truth', bringing us 'grace upon grace' (that is, more generously than we deserve or could expect: John 1.14–17). At the end of time as we know it, Christ will bring grace when he is revealed (1 Pet. 1.13). 'Grace' is a many-faceted, many-coloured word that encompasses the great theme of God's gift of Christ, and what it is that inspires God's people to carry on the work he has given us to do. Grace connects with everything that we are, and everything that we do, through God making those things possible. So too we give thanks that Christ has 'opened the gate of glory' because grace now, and hope for life in eternity, is centred on him and what he has done.[40]

Live his risen life

By grace, our outlook and understanding about life and what it means are changed. What we see now, in the present and from our human perspective, 'isn't all that there is'. Living Christ's risen life

---

40 For a brief discussion of hope for eternity see the previous chapter.

now means knowing that Jesus Christ is risen, that human life is infinitely precious in God's sight, and that 'if we have been united with him in a death like his, we will certainly be united with him in a resurrection like his' (Rom. 6.5); it means not having our horizons confined to the present and the world as it is. It means living and working in a way that anticipates, so far as possible, how things are when God is unequivocally and visibly in control. Although the resurrection of all people is in the future,[41] Jesus' resurrection is already a fact, and we are to see ourselves so closely united with Christ's death and rising through baptism that it makes sense to speak of living risen life now:

> [I]f you have been raised with Christ, seek the things which are above ... Set your minds on things that are above, not on things that are on earth, for you have died, and your life is hidden with Christ in God. When Christ who is your life is revealed, then you also will be revealed with him in glory. (Col. 3.1–4; see also Col. 2.12 and Rom. 6.4)

Paul and other writers encouraged the first generation of Christians to live in the light of Christ's resurrection. But they were careful to make it clear that accepting the good news of Jesus' victory over death was not a reason to sit back and do nothing except wait passively for God to bring his kingdom in all its glory. Far from it: this world had to be lived in with Christian integrity. They had a mission to tell its people about what God had done, and would yet do, through Christ. They were to live in a way that witnessed to the fact that they were God's people. The everyday life of the Christian community should be Christlike (in 1 Cor. 1 Paul contrasts the importance of this with the pettiness of getting involved in disputes and factions) and mutual love should be evidence that the disciples are genuinely Christ's followers (John

---

41 An early misapprehension on this point is corrected by 2 Timothy 2.18.

13.35). Among the New Testament writings that make the point is the first letter of John: '[L]et us love, not in word or speech, but in truth and action ... And this is [God's] commandment, that we should believe in the name of his Son Jesus Christ and love one another, just as he has commanded us' (1 John 3.18, 23). For the writer of that letter, belief and love cannot be separated. To believe in Christ means to recognize his love; and that love is only authentic and worth the name if we are prepared to do the (sometimes hard) work of loving. Love in the Christlike sense is generous and imaginative love that recognizes and celebrates the image of God in others. It is meaningless to pray, 'he declared your love', unless we are ready to reflect and imitate love of that kind in the situations where God puts us.

Discipleship and integrity

As we pray that 'we who drink his cup [may] bring life to others; we whom the Spirit lights give light to the world', we are affirming that faith is personal but it is not self-serving. How do we bring life to others? The thrust of the New Testament is that life is the gift of *God* through Christ (John 10.10), and the suggestion in the prayer that it is *people* (and specifically we ourselves) who bring life to others is, at face value, daunting or at least rather odd. The key to this is to see the prayer as a hope and pledge that we will be living advertisements for authentic faith in the life-giving Christ. The prayer becomes a commitment to be bearers of good news, that is (literally) evangelists. But implicit in those words is a call to have a good dose of humility and self-awareness. It is fine to give thanks for what God has done for us, and in and through us, and it is absolutely right for practising Christians to want to share faith and to see a living faith grow in other people. But 'we whom the Spirit lights' will be unconvincing if that light is showing little effect. The most sophisticated theology and the most fervent clinging to all the words of the creeds will not do much to advertise the Christian faith if we who practise it are mean-spirited and hypocritical. If there ever was an age when the Church could assume that it would have authority in society at large merely because it *was* the Church, that certainly is not the case now. Christians should not be afraid of having to rise to the task of being able to demonstrate that the Gospel has made a difference to our lives, and that we work at making the common life of the visible Church worthy of a company that bears Jesus' name. Our first forebears in the Christian faith had to do exactly that, after all.

Freedom and praise

The line 'keep us firm in the hope you have set before us' encourages us to think of 'hope' as an aspect of God's plan that is sure, but that has not yet been made completely clear to us.[42] The prayer expresses the outcome of this hope in terms that 'we and all your children shall be free, and the whole earth live to praise your name'. It would be easy for that phrase to pass us by as a fine-sounding conclusion – it is after all full of words with comforting and positive associations. But it would be a poor deal if we were to end the Eucharist with platitudes. So, can we pray those words with integrity and truly mean what we say?

Looking to an ideal, and expressing it in terms of the future, is nothing new. It goes back to texts such as Isaiah 11 and 35. But holding to an ideal must energize dealing with the present. Discipleship demands that injustice, oppression and exploitation be recognized, challenged and reformed, as the tradition of addressing injustice in God's name goes back to the age of the prophets.

So when we pray that we and all God's children may be free, we need to think what we are committing ourselves to: working so that they may be free to *do* what, free to *be* what, and free *from* what? What we can do depends a great deal on our own situation.

---

42 On hope, see the previous chapter. The original *Series 3* version of this line was in rather less 'churchy' (cautious?) language: 'keep us in this hope that we have grasped'.

We may personally be in a position to affect other individuals' conditions directly; or we may have influence in a more indirect sense, through the choices we make when we shop or when we make gifts to charity. And while we might think of freedom immediately in terms of liberation from oppression and poverty, we need to recognize that, even in the most liberal and prosperous of societies, there are many people who feel themselves to be far from free. Individuals' lives are confined, restricted and hampered in a host of ways; people feel powerless when they are bullied or when they cannot access fair treatment. Many are held in contempt and are put at a disadvantage because of who and what they are. We need to face the questions: what is our part in any of this? And what can we do to change the experience of even one person for the better?

The whole earth

And what about praying that the whole earth may live to praise God's name? Perhaps originally those words would have evoked an image of all *humankind* being in a relationship of love and wonder towards God. But they resonate differently now, even from the time when they were written a few decades ago. It is probably true to say that, until comparatively recently, public opinion was not much bothered by what humanity together might have done, or be doing, to the planet. Even for those who deny that there is such a thing as human-generated climate change, the issue can't be ignored; habitats have been changed or destroyed in order to meet the interests that we are virtually all complicit in, as consumers even if not as industrialists or politicians. There is a strand of theology that queries the humanity-centred ('anthropocentric') assumptions of much of our thinking, preaching and praying. It suggests that the creation stories of Genesis are far better honoured by humanity exercising the stewardship and management that only we can, than by a use of animals, plants and minerals that is careless of the long-term effect of what we do. If the whole earth is to praise God's name, if we are to echo the words that 'God saw everything that he had made, and indeed, it was very good' (Gen. 1.31), then humanity has to treat the earth as a sign of God's glory, and neither cynically exploit it nor ignore the consequences of our actions and choices for future generations.

Praying this prayer and remembering our baptism

In this prayer, we are saying to God that we are lost without him; we have hope in him; we live by him; and we will work for him. There's a parallel between these themes and some that we meet in baptism. These words from the baptism service remind us that everything we do as Jesus' disciples springs from our identity in the company of those who have been made his own through baptism:

> The God of all grace, who called you to his eternal glory in Christ Jesus, establish, strengthen and settle you in the faith ... God has delivered us from the dominion of darkness and has given us a place with the saints in light. You have received the light of Christ; walk in this light all the days of your life. Shine as a light in the world to the glory of God the Father.

We can see our post-communion thanksgiving as a hope and pledge that we will have what we need to live out our shared calling (or 'vocation'). All this is held together, then, with our being joined to Christ in baptism, and fed by him in the Eucharist.

To think about further

How can the values that underpin our sharing in Holy Communion be lived out, once we have left the time and place of church worship?

21

A conclusion

Great is the mystery of faith

'Without any doubt, the mystery of our religion is great,' proclaims
1 Timothy 3.16:

> He was revealed in flesh,
> vindicated in spirit,
> seen by angels,
> proclaimed among Gentiles,
> believed in throughout the world,
> taken up in glory.

And in the eucharistic prayer, the words 'Great is the mystery of
faith' are the cue for everyone to say:

> Christ has died:
> Christ is risen:
> Christ will come again.

We have met the word 'mystery' already in Chapter 19. It occurs a
few times in the New Testament, and, out of those, three will help
us to understand its meaning within the context of faith better.
One comes from the Gospels, where Jesus tells his twelve disciples: 'To you has been given the mystery of the kingdom of God,
but for those outside, everything comes in parables' (Mark 4.11).
The second comes from the letter to the Colossians: 'I want [Jesus's
followers'] hearts to be encouraged and united in love, so that they
may have all the riches of assured understanding and have the

knowledge of God's mystery, that is, Christ himself' (Col. 2.2). And the third comes from a passage where Paul is explaining to the Corinthians that the Christian message is based on God's power and not human understanding. He writes: 'We speak God's wisdom, hidden in mystery, which God predetermined before the ages for our glory' (1 Cor. 2.7).

The point of these passages, and others in the New Testament that mention mystery, is that God enables us to grasp enough of the truth for us to be able to live in faith. 'Gnostic' religions, of the kind that were being practised at the time when the New Testament was being written, were based on invented secrets or mysteries that were only told to 'insiders': the New Testament writers' approach is totally different. God chose to reveal himself; and the key to understanding that is not secret ceremonies, and not fables, but the real person of Jesus Christ (1 Cor. 2; Col. 1.9–20; 1 Tim. 4.7; Heb. 1). Christian truth is, as it were, an 'open secret': open to anyone who sees that God is at work in Jesus' life, death and rising, and in the activity of the Spirit.

So 'Great is the mystery of faith' is saying something very different from 'religion is a great big puzzle that we can't start to comprehend'. It is saying: 'God has shown us wonderful truths.' Central to our faith are the events that took place at a specific time and place – Jesus' death and resurrection. And coupled with them is the belief, rooted in the time of Jesus and the first generation of Christians that produced the New Testament, that God has a plan for all things ultimately to be made subject to him: a belief summarized as 'Christ will come again' (Matt. 24.30; Rev. 1.7). Faith means going further than accepting that the events related in the Scriptures took place: it relates to what these events mean, why they are significant, and what difference they make to the business of living daily life.

The Christian faith is not the product of abstract theorizing or empty speculation: it comes from reality and experience. The early Christians, including the New Testament writers, realized that they stood in a unique place in human history: because in their own age God's relationship with humanity had entered a new phase, both through the things that Jesus had done, and through who he was. A small number had had the exceptional privilege of walking and talking with Jesus, asking him questions, learning from him and receiving his love at first hand: they had seen something of those things, too many to record, that Jesus had done (John 21.25). As the young Church spread out, it was always that sense and assurance of an authentic encounter with God, through word of mouth originating with the Apostles and then through the written Scriptures, that lay at the heart of faith.

When we approach Christian belief, two thousand years on, we are invited to make our mind and heart open for God to build our faith on the same foundations. Paul's trio of faith, hope and love (1 Cor. 13) speak strongly here. *Faith* is about a relationship of trust with God, before ever it is to do with propositions, forms of words, and creeds. *Hope* is about confidence in God's purposes, especially the elements of them that are beyond our powers to understand: and hope is what encourages Christians to maintain integrity amid difficulties of all sorts, including the loud voices that say religious faith is irrational, empty or even harmful. And the Christian faith looks to *love* – generous, mutual and self-giving which Jesus perfectly embodies – as the best possible description of 'how God is', the clearest explanation of why humanity exists, and the reason among all others why Jesus Christ lived and died and rose again. But to be a Christian disciple is also to acknowledge, and sometimes experience, how costly that Christlike love can be.

To answer the question 'Why believe?' with the response 'Because of love' is not to retreat into shallow sentimentalism. Nor is it to shy away from the fact that the Church – and particular individuals on its behalf – do work hard with the intellectual aspects of Christian belief, giving theology the academic serious-ness it deserves. To place love, given, received and returned, at the centre of belief is to remind ourselves of priorities that run through the Bible and in God's calling to the Church. We love because he first loved us (1 John 4.19). If exploring faith and studying the Bible and Christian worship convince us of nothing else, the task will have been well worth it.

For further reading

Piotr Ashwin-Siejkowski, 2010, *Early Christian Doctrine and the Creeds*, London: SCM Press.

John Barton, 2009, *What is the Bible?* (3rd ed.), London: SPCK.

Mark Earey, 2002, *Liturgical Worship*, London: Church House Publishing.

David F. Ford, 1999, *Theology: A Very Short Introduction*, Oxford: Oxford University Press.

Paula Gooder, 2009, *This Risen Existence: The Spirit of Easter*, Norwich: Canterbury Press.

Alister McGrath, 2007, *Christian Theology: An Introduction* (4th edn), Oxford: Blackwell.

Ben Quash and Michael Ward (eds), 2007, *Heresies and How to Avoid Them*, London: SPCK.

Kenneth Stevenson, 1998, *The Mystery of Baptism in the Anglican Tradition*, Norwich: Canterbury Press.

Rowan Williams, 2007, *Tokens of Trust: An Introduction to Christian Belief*, Norwich: Canterbury Press.

N. T. Wright, 2003, *The Resurrection of the Son of God*, London: SPCK.

Tom Wright, For Everyone, New Testament series, London: SPCK.

Tom Wright, 2006, *Simply Christian*, London: SPCK.

Tom Wright, 2010, *Virtue Reborn*, London: SPCK.